# Arturo's Dream

World Children's Transplant Fund
17404 Ventura Boulevard, 2nd Floor
Encino, CA 91316
WCTF.ORG

World Children's
Transplant Fund

# Arturo's Dream

*Elizabeth Seraphin and Robert Mummey*

*Library of Congress Cataloging in Publication Date*

Authors Elizabeth Seraphin and Robert Mummey
Title: Arturo's Dream
ISBN-13: 9781522895411
ISBN-10: 1522895418
Library of Congress Control Number: 2015921224
CreateSpace Independent Publishing Platform
North Charleston, South Carolina

*Printed in the United States of America*

*Watercolor by E. Seraphin*

*WE TELL OURSELVES STORIES*
*IN ORDER TO LIVE*

JOAN DIDION

# Contents

# CHAPTER 1

# The Phone Call

FROM THE INSIDE OF MY coat pocket, the buzz from my cell phone was loud and clear.

*Should I answer it? I suppose I should.*

At the other end of the line, in her typically flat voice, was the stable girl who was riding horses with Amanda that Monday.

"How are you?" I asked.

She and Amanda trained at Galway Downs in Temecula, eighty-five miles south of Los Angeles, California, a remote fifty-five-acre rambling horse ranch lined with hundreds of towering gray-green eucalyptus. Dusty California oaks provided shade from the blistering afternoon sun in chaparral, bouldered land. Well-kept stables, a racetrack, a cross-country course, and footpaths were spotted around little hillocks of manicured grass. White-painted railed fences bordered the grounds as far as one could see. I envisioned the vastness of the ranch in my mind's eye.

"So, how's it going there today in Temecula?" I asked, wondering if they'd had a flat tire or car trouble. *Well, there goes dinner.*

Like a recorded message, she stated with no emotion, "I'm calling because Amanda's had an accident."

Pressing the phone hard to my ear, I asked, "Is she OK?"

Although Amanda had been to the emergency room for the usual childhood bumps and bruises, I felt a sharp pang. My internal sonar searched for clues in this woman's monotone voice.

"She was riding her horse over a low rail when her horse tripped. Amanda was thrown to the ground, and the horse fell on top of her."

On occasion, riders might be injured when they'd fallen off or been thrown from their horses. I needed details.

*"How is she?"*

Silence.

"I *need* to know how she is."

As if she hadn't heard a word I'd said. Her silence left me feeling something more was wrong.

"Oh, when I called 911, I didn't know the ranch's address for the paramedics. Two strangers were walking across the far end of the field, so I ran and yelled out for help. They knew the address. They knew where we were."

Bristling and bewildered, my panic grew. *"How* is *Amanda? How* is *she?"*

Silence again.

Suddenly, a man's voice came over the cell phone. "I'm the paramedic. I'm here with your daughter. She had an accident. She's bleeding a lot."

I had enough of my wits about me to ask, "Where is the blood coming from?"

"There's a lot of bleeding from her ears, her nose, and mouth...especially from her ears. She's not conscious. You may want to meet us at the Temecula Community Clinic. Here are the directions."

"I am leaving right now!"

Another sharp pang struck me as the call ended. I had to get to the hospital...I'd deal with my fear later. The call ended.

There I stood in the lobby of Marie Callender's, amid lively conversation, with customers waiting to be seated, paying their bills, and ordering food to go. The aroma of warm corn bread permeated the restaurant.

It all vanished into a dark spiraling vortex in a single beat of my heart.

I was alone. Somehow I found the way to my car in the parking lot.

I threw the dinner bags of hot chicken, hamburgers, and corn bread into the car's trunk. Gripping the steering wheel, I had to be careful and not let anything go wrong in the mile drive to my house.

Pulling into my driveway and running into my house, I found Santos, my twenty-three-year-old nephew who was living with me, studying for his college exams at the dining-room table. Amanda and Santos were very close cousins.

"Amanda had an accident. Can you drive me to the Temecula Community Clinic?" I burst out.

Seeing my flushed face and hearing my tightened voice, Santos asked no questions as he caught the car keys I tossed to him. Without locking the front door, we jumped in the car, buckled up, and left my neighborhood heading for the freeway.

## HEADING EAST

Moving at a snail's pace, heading east from Los Angeles in rush-hour traffic would be a three-hour drive, with luck. It was stop-and-go until we left Los Angeles.

My heart was pounding a mile a minute, and my thoughts raced even faster.

Santos drove and fielded phone calls to our family. First, he called my mother, Grandma Janet Mummey, a women's rights attorney and vice president of the Los Angeles County Women's Commission. His next call was to Kristen, Amanda's older sister, who then called her father, my ex-husband.

Cell phone pressed to my ear, I spoke with the doctor at the Temecula Community Clinic, who said, "Amanda has just been airlifted to Riverside Regional Hospital." Reassuring words. "She'll leave this clinic for a larger hospital."

"She'll receive the very best treatment, won't she, Doctor?"

"The hospital has all the information you'll need," he added in a noncommittal voice.

Getting nothing further from him, my need to reach Amanda was overwhelming. I was frantic to be at her side.

Santos navigated the clogged traffic. I began to mutter to myself. "Amanda's in good health. She's strong. Her mother's coming and will take care of everything. She's had injuries before. Being airlifted is a sign of hope. Everything's going to be fine."

This was my mantra I said over and over again.

"She's in good health. She's strong. Her mother's coming and will take care of everything. She's had injuries before. Being airlifted is a sign of hope. Everything is going to be fine."

My body continued slowly rocking back and forth, back and forth, in the passenger seat. My arms tightly folded reassuring myself over and over.

"She's in good health. She's strong. Her mother is coming and will take care of everything. She's had injuries before. Being airlifted is a good sign of hope. Everything is going to be fine."

With one hand gripping the steering wheel and the other clutching his cell phone, Santos turned his head toward me and said, "Kristen thinks you might be exaggerating, as you sometimes do."

"Kristen is right. Sometimes I do." Their entire lives, my daughters have been extremely close and protective of one another and knew me well.

Yes, I did exaggerate at times. This reminder was like a lifeline tossed to me in a turbulent ocean. I regained my footing. Things *couldn't* be as bad as I made them out to be.

Rocking back and forth in the car soothed and distracted me. I began to ascribe magic to little things. A red stoplight.

When the signal turned from green to red, it meant we had plenty of time. *There's no rush. Amanda's OK. We'll reach her in plenty of time! Won't we?*

## EMERGENCY ROOM

Finally, we arrived at Riverside Regional Hospital. I rushed from the car into the main entrance, through two large glass doors, only to be told, "You're in the wrong place. The emergency room is at the far end of the hospital." The receptionist did not bother to look up. She pointed with an outstretched arm and stiff finger.

We ran back to the car and sped through the hospital's parking lots until we reached a big red sign that read Emergency Entrance. I jumped out at the curbside.

What forced me to slow down and fast-walk to the lobby?

Old superstitions began to warn me: if you walk under a ladder, it was bad luck. If you stepped on a crack, you'd break your mother's back. If you shattered a mirror, you'd have seven years of hard luck. Running through this lobby could bring unknown punishment.

Inside, families huddled. Some people cried, some read papers, some drank coffee, and some slept or stared with blank expressions of hope or despair. The lobby was packed with leaden faces.

Pushing through and passing by a nurses' station to an unmarked door, I found myself in a corridor—no signs, no arrows, and no directions. It must have been what Alice felt on the other side of the looking glass.

*Where am I?*

Behind me, a nurse yelled, *"You're* not *supposed to be here! You're* not *supposed to be here!"*

*This is where I belong—with my daughter. This is where I have to be. Who in the hell can say this to me? I will drag this yelling nurse to hell with me if I have to.*

She kept yelling. I saw two large stainless-steel doors, by chance, opening into the ER.

Inside, another voice commanded, "*Leave* now! Leave now! You *cannot* be in here!"

Pushing a cart filled with medical supplies, another nurse heard the commotion and looked my way. I met her glance and demanded to know: "Is that my daughter? Is that my daughter?"

I was pointing to a set of small orange-painted toenails peeking out from under a white sheet in a cubicle formed by a drawn curtain.

She saw the ferocity in my face and ordered her staff, "Let her by. Leave her alone. She's the mother of the girl we just admitted."

*Finally,* there was Amanda, lying quietly on a gurney.

Leaning over, I saw that her face and arms were scrubbed and cleaned, her hair was brushed, her cheeks were flushed, and she had new sun-kissed freckles on her nose. I felt her warm, fresh breath on my cheek; I smoothed her long hair and felt the gentle warmth of her skin. I delicately kissed her forehead and touched her cheeks, yet not wanting to disturb her sleep. Amanda was intact, uninjured, no black-and-blue marks, no bleeding—just my beautiful daughter. She was perfect—as perfect as the day she was born.

The pang dulled, the pounding in my chest quieted, and the magic and the superstitions slinked back into their wretched corners. Vanished. Gone.

With a sense of relief, I was able to walk over to the nurses' desk to get answers about Amanda's condition. They didn't add anything to what the paramedics had said.

Back at her bedside, holding her warm hand, touching her long, slender fingers, and rubbing her arm, I leaned over and whispered in her ear.

"Amanda, don't try too hard, but if you can hear me or feel me, squeeze my hand." She did. A little.

I whispered in her ear: "I love you. I am here with you. I won't ever leave you."

*Ah, we can work with this,* I thought. *She'll be OK. Nothing more can go wrong. She'll receive treatment and be released soon enough. This will all be in the past—forgotten—with more Big Mac runs to come and horse tails and her own hair to braid. After a good rest, Amanda will be polishing her boots and saddle to a high luster for next week's jumping competition in Temecula.*

Looking up, I saw Amanda's name had been handwritten in red marker on a white grease board in the center of the ER. She was at the top of the list. This meant she'd receive special treatment, I was sure.

Amanda had been in the ER for four hours. It was evening when I met Dr. Cantando, Amanda's attending neurologist. We exchanged a few words, and he hurried upstairs. Later, we learned that he alone cleaned, swept, and mopped the floor, and he arranged for Amanda's bed and medical equipment in the adult intensive-care unit's room 132. He did this to hasten Amanda's transfer and treatment. This was special treatment, indeed.

Dr. Cantando explained to me that Amanda had suffered a traumatic brain injury (TBI) as a result of her horse accident. As the two-thousand-pound animal attempted to right itself, it stepped on Amanda's head, fracturing both her skull and her helmet. For the next seventy-two hours, she'd be monitored and under his close observation at which point he would decide if surgery was necessary.

*How could this be if she was wearing a standard riding helmet?*

Kissing Amanda on her forehead and whispering, "Goodnight, Amanda. I'll be sleeping close by," I walked to the dimly lit empty AIC waiting room. Why was I grateful for the emptiness? The seating consisted of only a few metal chairs, so I lay down on the linoleum floor and found a used telephone book for a makeshift pillow.

My mother—Grandma Janet—and Kristen arrived from Santa Monica that afternoon. Leaving the hospital later that evening, Grandma Janet saw me lying on the linoleum floor and said, "Here, take this white coat I'm wearing. You'll need it to stay warm. I wish I could do more." My mother laid her coat over me, kissed my forehead, and left.

Hospital policy did not permit family members to stay overnight with patients. For her to hear my voice and feel my touch, I believed she would receive my healing energy. By being near Amanda, I could be transmitting a mother's prayers and spirit.

We both slept alone that night. She slept in her bed. My bed was the linoleum floor in the AIC unit's lobby. I cradled fears in this room of no exits. My fitful night's sleep incubated demons and despair.

The next morning, with hospital night-lights still on, I walked to the restroom. Outside was an early gray dawn and a blurry orange sunrise. In the small washroom, in the mirror , I saw a stranger whose eyes looked utterly lost. *For God's sake, get a grip*, I said to myself. *Pull yourself together. These are hard days. You have to be 100 percent there for Amanda. Now! Do it now! Shut out the demons. Push them far away. Make them go away.*

Feeling trapped, without exit or escape, I covered my mouth with my hands to fight back a howling scream—yet I had no voice, had no tears, and made no sound. There was no one to hear me anyway.

Tuesday morning, back in room 132, I kissed Amanda good morning and noticed her sea-green eyes hadn't changed. They were still open, unblinking, wide, and staring at the wall.

A nurse came in to check her pupils with a penlight.

"How is she?" I asked.

"I'm checking her eyes. She has a fixed stare, which we call 'doll's eye,'" and went on to describe the condition in medical terms. I nodded as though I understood. The nurse turned and left the room. My mind's eye flashed back to the summer of 1955, in my Grandmother Apple's fourth-floor attic, in the Bellow's house in Frankfort, Michigan. She had a world-class collection of antique dolls dressed in pinks and plaids with frilly laced collars, fluffy crinoline skirts, and gingham dresses with matching bonnets. On their little feet and hands, their nails were painted rosy reds and pinks. Satin slippers or silk shoes were worn by each doll and each doll's hair was tightly curled or tied with pink ribbons. Porcelain painted eyes blinked when the doll was tilted. When held back to a sitting position the doll's eyes returned to a perpetual, fixed stare.

Never ask what "doll's eye" means. Never!

I sat alone with Amanda in room 132. I sang quietly to her.

*Hush little baby; don't say a word.*
*Papa's gonna buy you a mockingbird.*

*And if that mockingbird don't sing,*
*Papa's gonna buy you a diamond ring.*

*And if that diamond ring turns to brass,*
*Papa's gonna buy you a looking glass.*

*And if that looking glass gets broke,*
*Papa's gonna buy you a billy goat.*

*And if that Billy goat don't pull,*
*Papa's gonna buy you a cart and bull.*

*And if that cart and bull don't pull,*
*Papa's gonna buy you a dog named Rover.*

*And if that dog named Rover don't bark,*
*Papa's gonna buy you a horse and cart.*

*And if that horse and cart fall down,*
*You'll still be the sweetest little baby in town.*

I must have sung it many times a day. It was all I could think of, all I could do.

Someone once said, "We tell ourselves stories in order to live." This was a singing story.

That night the nurse gave me a blanket and a small pillow. "Don't let anyone see you. It's against hospital policy," she said, so I curled up against the wall behind Amanda's bed, to be hidden but near her.

Hours later another nurse gently nudged me; it was like waking up "into the red eye, the cauldron of morning," as Sylvia Plath wrote—a haunting reminder to me.

"I'm taking Amanda to the hospital's basement for an MRI," she announced.

I vowed to myself to be there for all of Amanda's treatments and procedures.

She pulled out a plastic sheet and slid Amanda's 120-pound body from her bed onto the gurney. The nurse hooked up the heart rate and blood-pressure monitors and the green oxygen tank tucked next to Amanda's legs. The heavy black car-sized battery was hoisted up and anchored at her feet amid rumpled sheets. Secured by bars and railings.

My left hand grabbed the stainless-steel railing to help steer Amanda through the corridor toward an unfamiliar elevator. The nurse groaned under the weight of the gurney as we pushed it through the elevator doors. The elevator strained as we began our descent to the basement.

Within seconds, Amanda  bolted upright to a perfect sitting position, as if yanked like a marionette right out of her sheets. Instinctively, I reached over and held her shoulder.

*Oh God, it's going to be all right. She'll live. She'll ride again. Thank you, merciful God.*

Her back to me, holding the IV bottle on its stand, the nurse turned to see why I'd gasped.

Amanda began heavy projectile-vomiting, gushing red blood with a force that spattered the elevator walls and floor.

The frightened look on the nurse's face scared me. Stunned, I quickly turned and hid my face in the corner of the elevator, standing still as stone.

*Has an angry God scolded me for my arrogant hopes?*

The nurse struggled to lay Amanda back down, muttering, "I told that doctor she shouldn't be moved down here for an MRI."

Frantically, she hit the red button. As the elevator jerked and swayed, it returned us to where we'd started several minutes ago. Quickly we yanked the bloodied gurney out of the elevator onto the main corridor of the AIC.

"Code blue! Code blue!" burst out over the intercom.

*It must be for another patient! Amanda just needs to get cleaned up.*

Indistinguishable white coats poured out of patients' rooms. They rushed to Amanda, abruptly encircled her, stood still, and watched in silence. Until one resident jumped on top of her gurney, straddling Amanda's chest with his hands clasped and arms straight. His rapid, precise up-and-down movements pumped life into her. In the silence of this amphitheater of professional onlookers, I only heard his labored breathing. After an eternity, he stopped, took a deep breath, raised his right hand, and commanded the nurse, "Call the time."

"Doctor, the time is eleven twenty a.m."

White coats milled around, uttering medicalese in soft voices. Mocked by the clock's relentless ticking, never to be reset, the hand of time moved on.

There lay the sunshine of my life, swept off this earth with a simple pronouncement from a mechanical timepiece on a wall. I was numb and confused.

Alerted by the call for code blue, the hospital chaplain appeared immediately at my side. He laid his hand on my shoulder and offered to say the Lord's Prayer with me. Infuriated, I turned on him. "No, I don't want to pray with you! I haven't given up hope, even though you have." I wanted to cut him to little ribbons.

Then, the hand of a social worker touched my arm—mumbling well-worn clichés, suggesting she could make a difference.

"What can I do for you?" she implored.

"Get that chaplain the hell out of here."

She quickly vanished, along with the chaplain.

I felt violated. They may as well have been circling vultures.

The resident doctor had just miraculously resuscitated Amanda, I believed. He spoke more medicalese to the nurse, further disorientating and alienating me. Amanda and I were now alone in the empty corridor with its polished linoleum floors and the undeniable antiseptic smell of the intensive-care unit.

Still not a single word was said to me—no explanation of the horror I had just witnessed. I was dumbfounded. A gray fog of denial slowly swirled around me. *Maybe this was not so bad.* Clinging to the cold steel railing of the gurney with its bloodstained sheets, blinking lights, and beeping monitors, I followed Amanda and her nurse back to room 132.

Amanda was cleaned up, dressed in a fresh gown, and lifted back into her bed, sheets tucked in on all four corners. Oxygen and IV were reconnected. The electrocardiogram, blood pressure, and electroencephalograph were plugged in—all read normal.

*She must be OK.*

These blinking colored lights transported me to our last Christmas Eve together, three months earlier. A sprained ankle prevented me from driving, so one evening Amanda showed up at my front door.

"Mom, we're going to see the Christmas lights and decorations. I'll drive us to the Santa Monica Pier to see the sights." The night was clear and cold. Only a few last-minute shoppers were out. What a nice surprise.

Traditionally, we enjoyed lighted nativity scenes built along the Pacific Palisades Bluffs, silhouetted against the dark Santa Monica Bay. For miles up the coast we delighted in seeing the twinkling lights locals called "the String of Pearls." We drove slowly through ocean-side streets under a shower of sparkling Christmas colors of greens, reds, and golds beneath a pale winter moon. We were touched by the brightly lit nativity scenes depicting Jesus's life from birth to resurrection. Amanda had brought a blanket to cover my legs, so I was tucked warmly inside the car. We chatted leisurely about Amanda's boyfriends, high-school classes, and friends—the usual girl talk.

I was pulled back to Amanda's bedside by the blinking lights of the hospital machines.

Relatives and friends began to arrive: Kristen; Grandma Janet; Santos; Adrian, my brother; and his wife, Carmen, who brought food, snacks, and drinks. Several of Amanda's girlfriends and Amanda's boyfriend were also with us. By afternoon, my sister, Christine, from New Orleans, Amanda's father from Hermosa Beach, her uncle from Massachusetts, and Cousin Kara from Michigan all joined us. Phone calls from family and friends continued throughout the day and evening.

It was a blur.

## THE MEETING

Late that evening, Amanda's neurologist, a thin gray-haired man, gathered us in a small waiting room adjacent to room 132. I felt comforted that Amanda was near. The adult intensive-care unit, on night status with lowered temperatures, was lit in a strange yellowish hue. Metal chairs with arm rests of wood-colored plastic—not comfortable but adequate—surrounded a low Formica coffee table in the center of the room. Glass walls from floor to ceiling enclosed us like goldfish in a bowl. Those who looked in could see tight facial expressions and hunched postures and ringing of hands.

*What's coming next? What is he doing?*

Before he sat down or said a word, his authoritative presence unsettled me. He was wearing a white lab coat, the business suit of doctors, with a photo ID pinned to his lapel. In his lab-coat pocket was a small ballpoint pen and penlight. A stethoscope hung around his neck like a noose. His glasses were firmly perched on his nose.

Reviewing the test results, notes, and doctor's observations with us, and referring to his notes in medical language, with a practiced smile, he said, "Two-thirds of Amanda's brain stem is not functioning. It never will. Amanda is not going to survive."

*This can't be happening.*

Santos fell out of his chair onto his knees and sobbed uncontrollably.

Kristen pleaded, "You are doctors. You have been to medical school. You have the training. Why can't you *fix* this?"

"Can't they regenerate from the other one-third, like a lizard's tail?" I begged. *I don't understand the doctor' words; they keep changing.* I never heard his answer. Grandma Janet and Adrian took the brunt of the news with little outward expression, stunned. Disintegrating, I had neither words nor tears. The doctor excused himself and left us alone.

Soon after, a young resident approached us.

"I should not be asking you this, but have you considered organ donation?" he asked us.

"No, I never thought about it."

Amanda's driver's license had no pink dot, which would have indicated she was an official organ donor. Both of my daughters were vigorous, healthy, and happy. Why would they need the pink dot?

Speechless, I didn't know what to say or where to turn.

"We want more time because this is happening so fast," said Bob, my brother, to the doctor.

I wanted to know what her sister and friends thought. What would Amanda want? In some ways, they knew her better than me.

Amanda's sister, friends, and cousins knew what Amanda would have wanted.

"Donation—she believed in it," they all answered without hesitation. "Remember, she was a caring and generous person. In honor of her friend Diane, she entered and finished the AIDS walk every year."

At 2:00 a.m., we met with the UNOS (United Network of Organ Sharing) representative from OneLegacy, a nonprofit organization responsible for coordinating organ donors with organ recipients. She arranged to meet us in the medical-staff lunchroom adjacent to room 132. Empty paper cups and half-drunken sodas had been left on the tables. Opened bags of chips and crumpled napkins littered the floor. The night janitors hadn't cleaned yet, so we pushed several square tables together to form a U shape so that we could see one another.

In clinical terminology, the OneLegacy representative explained the donation process. Her cold and detached manner led us to feel we didn't want to "make any donations." Bob spoke to OneLegacy, and a new representative was dispatched, with whom we were comfortable. I drifted in and out, numbed to decisions of donations. With little sleep and after some painful discussion, we decided that all of us had to agree on the donation of each organ, or the organ would not be donated.

A decision had to be made for each separate organ: donate or not donate. Donation form 128-B listed each organ. Next to the name of each organ were two small boxes: one for "yes" and one for "no." I didn't grasp what I was doing. Simply by marking a box, life was given or denied.

First listed were the lifesaving organs: the heart, then the lungs, followed by the pancreas, kidneys, intestines, and liver. On the right side of form 128-B, the life-enhancing organs were listed: corneas, eyes, blood vessels, skin, tendons/ligaments, bones from the upper arms, and bones from legs and pelvis. Blood types, antigens, organ size, and thirty-two other criteria were considered for a proper match. It was like checking off the items on a shopping list. Little pen marks were just that. They had no relationship to Amanda with her pink cheeks and warm hands lying in her room.

## DECEPTIVELY SIMPLE

The representative instructed us that the donation forms had to be completed and signed within hours. I didn't know why.

The clock had begun ticking, for each organ had limited viability. Amanda's heart was the first box to be checked. Even though each family member said yes, I had the last vote.

"Yes," I whispered. None of it mattered anyway. They told me it was the right thing to do. I acquiesced.

It was 3:00 a.m. when I gazed up at the wall clock. A cool air filled the lunchroom as we voted yes for her lungs. Decisions for each organ became more difficult.

As night moved on, so did the pain. Amanda lay twenty feet away.

Yes for the pancreas. Yes for the kidneys. The last lifesaving organ was Amanda's liver.

"Yes," I voted.

"It's like we're taking her apart piece by piece. I can't go on," someone said.

Gasping and crying, another family member burst out, "It is like we're dismantling her."

We tried and tried. Our family could go no further.

"Let's take a break," Bob said exhausted and numb.

During our break, we knew we had to stop.

"I can't give up her beautiful blue-green eyes." I believed the eyes are the windows to the soul. We were finished. The life-enhancing organs—eyes, skin, ligaments, and more—remained with Amanda.

These decisions though, irrevocable, would not haunt me but would haunt my brother forever.

At lightning speed, our transplant coordinator, Gregg, set up a work space at the nurses' station near Amanda's room—computers, phones, and faxes. His sole task was to locate compatible recipients throughout the United States and Canada. After several hours, he reported his findings but had to return to his station to broaden his search across the United States from west to east because of a lack of compatibility of recipients. As yet, his search did not meet with success.

My fear was Amanda's heart would be orphaned.

Gregg walked a fine line between communication with our family and his clinical work of data-mining abstract information. We had questions. We had comments. Totally fatigued, we sobbed and were silent.

For the first thirty-six hours, Gregg sat at his makeshift desk, searching for matches. The clock seemed to mock us, as the hands relentlessly move on. I felt the urgency of this race to unite Amanda with a recipient.

Room 132 became our bubble of isolation. Gregg understood. He suffered the loss of his younger brother. This made him one of us, with his caring eyes and soft-spoken manner. Every few hours, Gregg came to our room with disappointing and disheartening news.

"We still don't have a match for her heart," or, "The match was no good. It didn't work out."

For the next thirty-six hours, nothing changed. The green light of Gregg's computer cast an eerie glow on his face, leaning over his keyboard as he continued his search.

The symbolism of a heart, the spiritualism, and the magic are age old. Throughout history, hearts have been broken, hearts turned to stone, and hearts ached with love. Great poems were written about hearts. The heart is an icon. Hearts are carved into trees with lovers' initials.

We prayed that Amanda's heart would find a home and that the recipient would live as vigorous a life as Amanda had for her twenty-five years.

Time doesn't stop; no reset. Without judgment, the clock ticked on; precious time passed. Our hopes faded.

Her heart couldn't be orphaned.

Far away in Canada, clinging to life in his hospital bed, lay a small man. Gregg looked up from the computer and rushed into our room, excited.

It was 1:00 p.m. Friday afternoon when we heard the words we were aching to hear: "I found a match for Amanda's heart!"

At last!

Victory bound us together. We high-fived, cheered, and smiled out of happiness and a keen sense of relief, if only for a few moments. We had a kaleidoscope of feelings, everything from elation to agony.

"We have to move Amanda quickly," Gregg said as he rushed in, followed by two nurses. They lifted Amanda with her IVs and monitors from her bed on to a gurney.

Things began to happen fast.

But only a few days ago, Amanda had been riding a horse on a clear spring day without a care in the world. Now, I looked at her lying on a bed with white sheets. Her cheeks were warm and rosy; I wanted her to get up and ride again.

With only minutes for a last prayer, I laid rosary beads across her heart intertwined with fresh poppies. I kissed her still-warm cheek, knowing it would be my last time. Yesterday her sister had painted her toenails a velvety orange—the color of poppies blanketing the fields outside her window.

We exchanged smiles and high fives with the staff and nurses who had been our comrades in spirit for the past five days. They watched our victory parade as we walked from room 132 for the last time. Everyone laid a hand on Amanda's gurney to share the energy of her spirit and our love.

During my last few moments with Amanda, believing she might hear me, as some thought possible... I promised, "Amanda, we'll never be far apart from one another. You will be cherished forever. For a fleeting second, you'll return here and we'll find each other. We'll share a quiet place where small wonders and beauty of life will swirl. All you knew and loved will come in memories, in dreams, in visions, in instinct, in sensations, in imagination. From far away you may seek a comfort in the sound of wings fluttering, a night dappled in stars, the face of a daffodil, the scent of rain. As we have been together for 25 years, we will meet again for another 25 years.. or more".

Amanda was readied.

We weren't.

Above two tall steel doors a sign read "No Admittance— Operating Room." Gregg told us we couldn't go any farther. Slowly and silently these doors opened, and Gregg pushed the gurney through. The last thing I saw was Amanda's carefully brushed hair, flowing down.These doors slowly and silently closed as if swallowing her up.

For a moment we stood frozen in time, and we could not leave her or stop saying, "Good-bye, Amanda."

My mind had to take a perfect picture of her to last my lifetime.

Earlier that day, before Gregg finished his exhaustive search, we heard the whirling of helicopter blades cutting through the air of the clear afternoon sky. From our third-floor window, we turned toward the sound.

"Look, everyone, two helicopters are here for Amanda." Bob said.

In their cockpit, we could see the faces of the helmeted pilots as they flew over the  mountainside approaching us. I knew them, even though they did not know me.

The surgeons had to meet the 2:00 p.m. scheduled deadline for organ viability. Scheduling had to be precise for the doctors, medical staff, pilots, and ambulance drivers. Specialized teams of surgeons were required for removal and preparation for transportation of each organ.

The doctors for Amanda's lungs had flown in late Wednesday night from Minnesota. From Southern California Loma Linda Hospital, two transplant teams came in separate ambulances for two separate recipients; one middle-aged man from Lancaster, California, waited to receive Amanda's pancreas and kidney. Amanda's liver would go to a recipient from Corona, California.

At 1:00 p.m., Gregg located a heart recipient in Canada, but there was not enough time to fly a surgical team to the Riverside hospital. The Minnesota team, already at the hospital, volunteered to perform the surgery for Amanda's heart. One helicopter flew out to deliver the cooler with her heart to LAX, where a private jet was waiting to transport the cooler to a team waiting in Canada. The second helicopter flew to LAX to deliver Amanda's lungs, in a cooler, to a private jet bound for Minnesota. The helicopters lifted up into the night sky and vanished.

A few of us stayed to collect overnight bags, makeshift pillows, candy wrappers, emptied bottles of aspirin, sweaters, socks, and empty soda cans. Uncle Bob collected her gold earrings and put them into a shopping bag. Amanda's riding pants and shirt were torn and soaked with blood. Neither the hospital nor the ambulance would or could locate them. Her sister, Kristen, collected Amanda's jewelry and makeup. Grandma Janet picked up her own coat, which, by now, was no longer white. Adrian collected uneaten food.

No evidence of our stay could be found in room 132. The janitors might have seen signs of our presence when they unplugged, disengaged, and disassembled the monitors, the IVs, an EKG, and bedclothes. The room was stripped clean. I needed her belongings to be with me. I wanted to hold in my lap the remembrance of Amanda's presence.

Needing to see for myself, before returning with Santos to Los Angeles, something compelled me to drive behind the hospital and up a small hill to the helicopter pad. I wanted to feel the threads connecting Amanda to those points where her flights took her. Again, I snapped a vivid photo in my mind.

Into that bleak and bitter night, we drove west on the 91 freeway, north on the 405 for the last stretch.

CHAPTER 2

# After

*Happy families are all alike; every unhappy*
*family is unhappy in its own way.*

—LEO TOLSTOY, ANNA KARENINA

May 5, 2013   Dream
*I've lived in this house for twenty-five years. Bombs are dropping close to*
*me. I pull my car into the driveway, get out, and as always, yank out my*
*house keys. I count an exact number of steps up to the front porch. I reach*
*for the front door, open it, and press through. I look forward, but there is*
*nothing! Bombing? There is no house; there is no sign of a house. Nothing*
*to show the house was here; no signs of moving trucks, no for-sale signs,*
*no signs of demolition or evacuations. Grass has grown over the markings*
*of the foundation. I turn to leave and find the front door and front porch*
*have disappeared.*

*Neighbors walk by looking at my face with their watery eyes and move*
*on. But I ask them, "What happened here?"*

*They say, "You know what happened," but I don't. Where is my home*
*of twenty-five years, my comfort?*

*If I turn back quickly, one more time, my house might magically appear:*
*the solid three-dimensional house. This is the worst mistake.*

*At night I lay down in my house to sleep in the cool green grass where*
*the house has always been. It is where I belong.*

# A FUNERAL

A funeral needed to be planned. It seemed no different from arranging a party or event; invitations, food, music, guest lists, and logistics needed to be coordinated. I was detached and ambivalent; planning would have to take care of itself.

The next morning at the Santa Monica Mortuary in the Chapel of the Dawn, decisions had to be made. I selected a small wooden box with burnt etchings detailing a nameless young horse romping across fields. Simple and smooth, this earthen wooden box would cradle Amanda for eternity.

"*Mom, I love horses; I want that one,*" *Amanda told me.*

From the mortician's catalog, we chose a casket and prayer cards from among those displayed in the basement sanctum. In life, Amanda loved horses. In death, they'd be together forever in the wooden box. The mortician said this would be engraved on the box of her "cremains."

Amanda Katherine Seraphin
July 11, 1977–April 24, 2003

"Do not ever refer to my daughter as 'the cremains.'"

"This is only a legal terminology," he retorted.

"Don't ever refer to my daughter as 'the cremains'!" I replied angrily.

He did not respond. My Amanda would never be "cremains" in *any* terminology.

Outside the mortuary, something waited for me in the blinding sunlight.

From the Little Chapel of the Dawn, my daughter and I met at a stationery store in Santa Monica. Inside, clean glass cases held colorful samples of printed cards and stationery in fanned displays. There was something for every occasion; I veered toward one case with spring-colored, flowered, lacy borders. One in particular caught my eye, vibrant and youthful. I pointed it out. "This is the one—lavender and yellow—I like."

The clerk looked at me. After a slight pause, she gently led me to another case with rows of subdued colored cards. She explained softly, "The other ones are for weddings; let's look in another case where we have cards more appropriate for somber occasions such as yours." And we did.

Despite her suggestion, I selected pale-pink thank-you notes with a tiny riderless horse embossed at the lower corner of the card.

As the clerk wrote the order, I glanced again at the stationary, it appeared so colorful, airy, full of life.

*Oh, what a wedding she would have.* I lingered over those invitations, and imagined a "WHAT IF" wedding. It warmed me inside... ... ... .....*It was a beautiful, clear morning; a few wispy clouds floated above in a sky of cobalt blue. Amanda was a vision. A thin gold wreath of pink petals and bits of moss held back her hair. A small tendril slipped out. Down her back, strands of hair fell into a loose braid, baby jasmine tucked in here and there. Embroidered with lace her soft linen dress was hand- stitched in seed-pearls glinting in the sun. The aura around her was a radiant glow for what was to come.*

*Her hands held a bouquet of favorite field flowers; purple columbine, orange poppies, dried lavender, yellow daisies, and willow slips tinged with pink berries... stems wrapped in forest-green ribbons and streamers, for her special day.*

*With a light step, she walked down a path where the air was scented with lemon blossoms from a nearby grove. Continuing on, she reached an arbor recessed in trees, overgrown with vines of magenta bougainvillea. Surrounded by benches, a small pool gurgled and bubbled water from its spout. The benches invited her to rest awhile and in wait of the communion ceremony a satin bible lay near. Inscribed by her grandmother, it was open to a particular passage and she began reading. Later the afternoon sky deepened into layers of purple, lavender and pale yellow. Then the last light of day cast a golden hew before deepening to dark.*

*Proceeding on, she knew the way would be lit as crystalline chandeliers hung from the arms of large, oak branches; swaying in a breeze casting kaleidoscope patterns. Strands of tiny lights adorned the pathway she passed along. Far from all city noise and lights, she took a moment to rest against a thick oak. She had not yet reached her destination, but when she looked upward she knew it was within the trillions of stars.*

The clerk's voice interrupts: *"It's time to finish this order and write the checks...I don't mean to disturb you."*

I quietly tucked one piece of the wedding stationery into my pocket and walked out of the store. I gripped the piece tightly, secretly envisioning, secretly planning the "what if" wedding.

From there, we drove to the Santa Monica Parish to meet with the church coordinator, the cantor, the priest, the deacon, the pianist, and a family friend, the florist. During the meeting, my thoughts drifted back to late nights when I gently walked baby Amanda in my arms, patting her back to loosen her colic. I felt the grayness of an endless test pattern on TV. My mother, a dedicated parishioner, led the meeting; with her approval, plans were finalized.

Amanda's viewing was held in the Chapel of the Dawn. Her sister had searched all the way to Malibu for the perfect pink linen riding shirt for Amanda to wear. Her head rested on a soft silk pillow in the half-opened casket. Amanda showed neither signs of trauma nor signs that she was an organ donor.

Gazing at her laid out in the white fluffy pillow-lined casket, I didn't recognize my own daughter; I didn't look again.

The deacon invited us to pay our last respects. Amanda's father and I hugged. He said a few words from the podium. Then it was my turn. I could not speak openly, so I read a poem by Robert N. Test.

## To Remember Me

*The day will come when my body will lie upon a white sheet neatly tucked under four corners of a mattress located in a hospital busily occupied with the living and the dying, for all intents and purposes, my life has stopped.*

*Don't call this my deathbed. Let it be called the Bed of Life.*

*Give my sight to the man who has never seen a sunset.*

*Give my heart to a person whose heart has caused endless pain.*

*Give my blood to the teenager, pulled from the wreckage of his car so he might live.*

*Give my kidneys to one who depends on a machine to exist from week to week and my liver to one so deserving.*

*Someday a speechless boy will shout the crack of a bat and a deaf girl will hear the sound of rain against her window. Then scatter my ashes to the winds to help the flowers grow.*

*Give my sins to the Devil.*

*Give my soul to God.*

*If by chance, you wish to remember me, do it with a kind deed or word to someone who needs it. If you do all I have asked, I will live forever.*

Her funeral, the next day, was held at St. Monica's Church. There wasn't an empty pew within the vaulted cathedral. It was a celebration of Amanda's life. Soft pink roses lay atop the green mourning shawl embroidered in gold; a gold crucifix lay atop her coffin to protect her. Deacons handed out hymnals, spiritual readings, and Mass cards at each pew. Her Mass cards read:

In Loving Memory
Amanda Katherine Seraphin
July 11, 1977 to April 24, 2003

### *I'm Free*

*Don't grieve for me, for now I'm free.*
*I'm following the path God laid for me;*
*I took his hand when I heard him call*
*I turned my back and left it all.*

*I could not stay another day*
*To laugh, to love, to work, to play;*
*Tasks left undone must stay that way.*
*I found that peace at the close of day.*

*If my parting has left a void,*
*Then fill it with remembering joy,*
*A friendship shared, a laugh, a kiss;*
*Ah, yes, these things I too will miss.*

*Be not burdened by times of sorrow;*
*I wish you the sunshine of tomorrow.*
*My life's been full, I've savored much,*
*Good friends, good times, a loved one's touch.*

*Perhaps my time seemed all too brief,*
*Don't lengthen it now with undue grief.*
*Lift up your heart and share with me.*
*God wanted me now—he set me free.*

The pungent aroma of incense floated throughout the cathedral as the Monsignor led the procession up the marble stairs to the main altar. The pallbearers laid Amanda's coffin at the foot of the altar.

During Uncle Bob's eulogy, a brownish-gray sparrow flew from the vestibule up into the vaulted ceiling. This little bird captured everyone's attention.

Bob stopped, pointed up, and said, "Look, we have a little visitor. It must be Amanda. She's with us." Searching for the perfect place to view this ceremony of life, our little visitor landed on the altar's crucifix and then alighted and perched on a ledge high above the seated mourners. There it remained as our friend.

With the cantor's haunting version of "Just a Closer Walk with Thee," the ceremony ended. The little sparrow fluttered and flew away the same way she flew in.

## CLEARING OUT HER APARTMENT

Clearing out Amanda's apartment was a cruel exercise. Grandma Janet, Kristen and a friend, and I began the painful task of sorting through her personal and daily belongings. Grandma Janet took the bathroom and boxed Amanda's towels, her bathroom scale, shampoo, conditioner, toothbrushes, hairbrushes, and combs. The shower curtain, decorated with tropical fish, was folded carefully like a commemorative flag. The medicine cabinet, now bare, was emptied of all items used for her daily routines. Amanda's laundry, hamper with underwear, sheets, socks, and pillowcases, waited to be washed during our Monday rituals. Ten years later, that same basket with unwashed clothing remains untouched in my garage.

Her sister and her friend did the heavy lifting, disassembling her bed and mattress, and collecting her flowered sheets and pillows. Her party dresses, high heels, riding gear, coats, and scarves were gathered and carefully folded for storage in her suitcases.

In a stupor in Amanda's kitchen, I stood looking at spices in their rack. A coffeepot, plates, pans, a mop, two brooms, and a few cans of her favorite soups—chicken noodle and tomato and cat food—were packed into cardboard boxes. The empty cabinet doors were closed for good. Amanda was not a gourmet cook; she was a fast-food kind of girl.

Milk had spoiled; vegetables wilted. Fruits were spotted and brown. Kristen's friend, an engineer, calculated dimensions and measured her car to see what would fit. He arranged stacked cartons, making aisles for our easy passage and priority loading. He created a sense the world could be put back into order.

"What about Spanky and Cranky?" Her sister asked all of us.

Spanky and Cranky were two cats Amanda adored and had rescued from a shelter eight years ago. They had gone two weeks without much food or water. Searching the apartment, Kristen found them, frightened and hungry, hiding underneath Amanda's bed. With great care, she coaxed the cats from their hiding place into their travel carriers. They would come to live with me.

Bank accounts, bills, checkbooks, a passport, a driver's license, her diary, letters, and her cell phone stored in accordion folders. Next to the front door, Amanda hung a small grease board with a to-do list. Her last handwritten reminder before leaving for Temecula competition read as follows:

1. Get duplicate set of keys for Michael.
2. Get cat food.
3. Pay electric bill.
4. Gas for car.

Packing our three cars, I wrapped the to-do board in clear plastic and stored it there for years.

Leaving the cold, empty silence, I locked the front door behind.

## LETTERS

In 2005, I received letters from three organ recipients. As part of their policy, these letters were first sent to OneLegacy for review of confidentiality and anonymity; then forwarded to me in separate envelopes. The letters were surreal and seemed to have a life of their own; they were faceless and unknown to me. I resisted reading them but changed my mind several weeks later. What could they possible say?

Gregg, our transplant coordinator, sent a letter handwritten in ink on his personalized blue embossed stationery. Quickly, I stuffed the letters back into their envelopes and put them in a shoebox, returning them to the back of my closet—not to be read for five years.

October 16, 2003   Dream

*Amanda is eight years old; she has travelled to Europe. She sends a postcard with a dark background the faces of millions of people are pictured.*

*Amanda, in the foreground, wearing her little favorite summer striped dress. Her back is turned to me. She extends and outstretches her arms...her little arms are crooked at first and then elongate like an angel in exaltation.*

## THE DESERT SEARCH

Desperate to find Amanda, to hold her slender hand, talk with her, share a laugh, hear her voice—I resorted to a psychic. On busy Santa Monica Boulevard was a vaudeville marquee in bold orange neon flashing lights: "PSYCHIC READINGS." For years, I had paid no attention. This particular afternoon was different. Impulsively I made a hard right turn into the parking lot. My mother, Janet, and sister, Christine, were with me. A small red neon sign flashed the word "open."

A dark-haired, middle-aged woman in a multicolored robe with jeweled sleeves and turquoise earrings greeted us with open arms, as though we were family. After exchanging our first names, times available, and prices, I accepted her invitation. I followed her to a private room. Janet and Christine were asked to remain waiting in the foyer. She offered me a red-laced deep chair with huge arm rests.

"What brought you here? I see a deep sadness."

I was stunned by the possibility when she asked me several times, "Do you want to contact Amanda?"

"More than life itself," I replied with a nod.

"I know of an opportunity, if you are interested..."

"Absolutely!"

"Let me make a phone call. I'll be right back." The psychic left the room.

I was alone. All I thought about was hugging Amanda again. I was light as a feather.

Returning, "I talked to my spiritual adviser, who said a renowned soothsayer would lead a special séance only tonight in Palmdale Desert. With such short notice, they would include me for ten thousand dollars in cash; you *must* be there by 9:00 p.m. You will be with your daughter," she said with urgency.

My instructions were to contact her within the hour with money. In exchange, she would give me an address and directions. I never called.


## CEREMONY OF "HAPPY" PEOPLE

In the spring, to honor donor families, Grandma Janet, Santos, Kristen, Uncle Bob, and I were invited to a Dove Ceremony at UCLA's Covenant Hall. The auditorium was filled with several hundred people. After being greeted, we were escorted through a sea of tables covered with white linen, each with a basket of white spring flowers and a numbered placard. The tables were indistinguishable from one another except for the handwritten names on place cards. A section near the stage was reserved just for recipients. This was because I believed they were all alike, recounting their tales of new lives of joy and purpose. We, the grieving, were segregated into the back part of the room with boxes of Kleenex on each table.

A slide show projected larger-than-life photos of each of our loved ones. Amanda's photo projected on the twenty-five-foot-high screen stunned me.

One by one, the recipients took the podium. Each spoke exuberantly with gratitude about their new lives: walking again, skiing, hiking, dating, having families, getting married, building rose-covered cottages, and tending gardens.

*What am I doing here?*

I hated them all. I didn't want to see the wretched white doves flapping their wings when released from their cages, in celebration of the living. It was trite, silly, and self-serving. My red-hot anger surprised me. Keeping these thoughts and feelings to myself, I was appropriately polite. We exited as soon as possible.

*Everyone understands a grief but he that hath it.*

—WILLIAM SHAKESPEARE

## TREE OF LIFE

On a later occasion, a Tree of Life ceremony at Riverside Regional Hospital honored donors and their families. Along with the others, my mother and I stood facing this Tree of Life in the hospital's main corridor. Sculptured in copper with the inscribed names of donors on shiny-bronzed leaves, it was dignified and elegant in its simplicity. Around the room, facial expression suggested losses were recent. Each face told its own story. I saw myself in them.

The head of the hospital opened the ceremony. Each donor family member was recognized and called to the podium and presented with a polished bronzed leaf. My engraved leaf read "Amanda Katherine Seraphin 1977–2003." What an honor to select a branch and permanently attach her leaf. One prominent branch was eye level and easy to touch. I'd always know where she is in the Tree of Life; when someone has a location, we know they exist.

Amanda's presence was in the palm of my hand; I touched the smooth edges of the leaf. With a kiss, I placed Amanda on her branch. Branches reached the ceiling, giving an arterial sense of a living organism. The energy of these donors' souls radiated from the Tree of Life. Comforted, I was with my own kind.

After the ceremony, as though our presence gave her permission, the CEO of Riverside Regional told us of her tragedy. She said, "I haven't shared this with many people...my daughter died in a car accident here right in front of this hospital." I understood her! We now had a unique unspoken language that would be there.

Nurses, doctors, and other staff members spoke to us of their stories. One nurse was special. She was the one in the intensive-care unit that night who said, "I'll look the other way. I shouldn't be doing this," before pulling the curtains across the windows so I could sleep hidden on the floor next to Amanda's bed. Her acts were grand gestures of the human spirit. She was an angel in a white uniform; I hugged her tightly.

## GALWAY DOWNS

Months later, we met Mr. Alvaro, the owner and manager of Galway Downs, in his elegantly furnished office in Temecula. We sat in plush chairs with a view of trellises filled with blooming magenta bougainvillea. After Amanda's accident, he had gathered her riding boots and gloves, her cracked, bloodstained helmet, and her wristwatch, storing them in a brown paper shopping bag in the back room of his office.

"I can't look at it. Please get it out of here. Put it someplace where I can't see it," I pleaded to my brother.

Alvaro walked us around the ranch's training grounds to find the exact location of Amanda's accident. Place and location mattered to me. I expected to see yellow crime-scene tape marking the fatal spot in the cross-country arena. Hoof prints led us to that spot. We found deeply gouged earth, broken rails, and clumps of scrub brush with broken branches. The rail the horse had tripped over had been moved by a ranch hand to a remote location. We found evidence of scuff marks embedded in the wood rail.

## October 5, 2003   Dream
*At Will Rogers Park, Amanda and I wear yellow sweaters. She leaves for a while to go back to the barn and returns but has no time for me. The polo fields fill up with other sports and other people. Still no time for me. I tell Amanda. I feel hurt and angry. She stops—comes close.*

*Looking down, she says, "Mom there's something we need to talk about. There is something I need to tell you…we need to talk." I know what it is. I don't want to hear it. I return to the polo fields, where I am ushered out and taken to a foreign country.*

*In my dreams, I always visit Amanda. Unspoken rules prohibit conversation, but we know what the other is thinking. If I speak—if I question anything—she'll vanish, and I'll never see her again. I am so careful not to break the rules. We do things together sometimes in broad daylight and sometimes at night. Sometimes we go shopping for clothes. On one shopping trip, I buy her a pretty pink sweater; she thanks me without speaking.*

Why did I have such a desperate need to feel the sand, look up at the trees, sense the breeze blowing, and see and mark the spot where Amanda left this earth?

On several occasions, I watched Amanda on her horse completing her jump. I imagined what could have been…*would she move on to the next level of competition? Would she earn a ribbon?*

Then we gathered in a small family memorial, placing a bouquet of plastic flowers on the sandy spot. Plastic would last longer in the scorched dry heat of the river basin. Holding hands, I felt numb while saying a prayer but followed the rest of the family. They knew the damage. They knew the life that had been cut short.

## SONGS

My brother and I grew up in the San Fernando Valley with its abundant orange trees. In spring and summer, the air was filled with the scent of lemon blossoms. Walnut groves gave us handfuls of nuts to munch when we played in the fields of local ranches. Walking to school, we had cactus apples for the grabbing.

When we were children, our mother sang songs to us. One of her songs was "Red River Valley."

> *Oh they say you are leaving this valley taking*
> *your bright eyes and sweet smile away.*

In my child's mind, I saw a truck loaded with a family and their belongings driving out of the valley.

"Clementine" was another song my mother sang to us. Now I understood the songwriter's pain.

> *Oh my darling, oh my darling*
> *Oh my darling Clementine,*
> *You are lost and gone forever,*
> *Fell into the foaming brine*
> *Dreadful sorry, Clementine.*

The word "forever" is piercing.

## MUSIC

Although I didn't speak a word of Italian, music had a visceral sense in the Italian opera *Norma*. Renée Fleming's performance of the mournful aria "Casta Diva" went straight into my soul like an arrow.

Time passed, and I attended a piano, cello, and violin recital where they performed Piano Trio in G minor Op. 15. It was composed more than one hundred and fifty years ago by Bedrich Smetana (1824–1884), who lost a child. The world-renowned violinist Robert Davidovici also lost a child. His interpretation of the music spoke to me in a way I could not have imagined of the composer's anger, anguish, and isolation from the death of his own child. Only music, not words, could express this kind of loss.

## WASHING MACHINE

Driving back and forth on LA freeways from home to work filled the empty hours. I earned an additional credential, sat in meetings, attended workshops, and led a dual existence.

Crying would find its way of catching up with me at home. I'd rush to my laundry room, cover the top of the washing machine with a pillow, and sob uncontrollably—afraid that concerned neighbors would check on me. It was impossible to be polite at the front door while going through a hurricane of pain. The machine barrel rocked back and forth, lulling me. Clicks between cycles and sloshing sounds whirred in rhythmic settings. If emotions had settings, I wanted peace and mercy added to the final cycle. Grief can't be washed away.

Earnest, caring individuals attempted to console me with their own sincere and heartfelt stories. Early on, I learned it was up to me to console them. Was I a grief magnet?

## PRICE OF ADMISSION

Early on, Bob said, "Our family joined a unique club in which no parent ever wanted to be a member. The price of admission was a parent's worst nightmare." He believed Amanda's donations gave our family a rare gift—a treasure to be discovered. I didn't agree then!

Entering an ambassador volunteer program, he spoke to the public about our experience as a donor family. The first day of training was held in a large conference room in a Pasadena hotel. Together with organ recipients, sitting around a long U-shaped table, each person described a "happy" lifesaving story as an organ recipient. Bob's turn was last. He was the only person in the room from a donor family. Overwhelmed by feelings of isolation and loneliness, he finished his story in tears. He left, unsure of being an ambassador. Amanda's story was unique and important and the other side—the silent side, the dark side—needed to be told.

## Three-Minute Limit

Eventually, I met with a psychologist. She openly stated she wasn't equipped to treat deep grief—only marital issues and teenage addictions. I continued to drift, feeling there was no end.

"You don't yet know the full impact this has had on you," another psychologist reflected.

Stumbling into Compassionate Friends, a national grief support group, I met with local members in the activity room of a temple. Thirty metal folding chairs were arranged in a circle. One group leader reminded us we each had three minutes to talk about our losses.

Returning to the next meeting, I heard a story that stayed with me. A father, an acclaimed writer, described his daughter's death in graphic detail. While on vacation and having a father-daughter conversation, the two were hiking up a steep cliff in Hawaii, and she lost her footing. In horror and unable to reach her, he stood helplessly watching his daughter tumble to jagged rocks far below. He told us she wore beige shorts, a white blouse, and brown-cleated shoes that afternoon in June. His recollection of details and his pain were as fresh as they were... thirty-two years earlier. His tears still flowed. I learned grief never ends.

Another man lost his four-year-old sister to leukemia. He watched his parents remove all photos, all remembrances of her, from their house and never spoke of her again.

Still searching, I found a grief support group for a small number of parents who'd lost adult children. Our two-hour weekly meetings continued for several years. We were glued together by the horror of our losses. The deaths of our adult children were our common bond. Each child died differently—some by accident, some by disease, and some by suicide. The parents of children who were murdered belonged to a different group.

It was important to continue to honor Amanda and the others by staying in contact. Occasionally, we'd joke about whose kids would get along with one another up in heaven. This kind of make-believe was comforting. The group helped stabilize and I continued to participate for several years. Like nomads crossing an endless desert in his or her own way and time, each of us survived.

Our group leader published a book about dealing with death and how we process it. She never addressed organ donation. I asked her why. "I never thought about it," she replied.

MAKING CONTACT

One mother who had also lost her daughter sensed my desperation. She offered the name of an acclaimed medium from England. He would be in Los Angeles for a few days. I needed to set up a session. After calling his New York office several times, I reached his assistant. She instructed me, "You need to send an eight-hundred-dollar cashier's check before we can schedule a session with Mr. Brown."

Taking a day off from work, I purchased a cashier's check at the bank and sent it through overnight delivery to Mr. Brown's secretary in his New York office.

Two weeks later, his assistant left me a cryptic phone message with two dates from which to select a session.

*Was I entering a secret world? Would I get ripped off again like the psychic tried to do? Am I grasping at straws? Am I a little crazy? Does it even matter?*

Two months later, with my brother for support, I attended a session with Mr. Brown in Redondo Beach. It started right on time, down to the minute. The medium's office apartment offered comfortable chairs and water but little else. There was a sense of transience.

"What do you want from our session?"

He gave a brief overview of what to expect during our "journey in spirit." Amanda's name was repeated over and over by the medium as he channeled, saying, "Amanda has this message for you: 'Mom, you'll be fine. I know you love me. You need to know I'm all right here in the spirit world. You know I love you and always will. Don't worry about me. Live your life.'"

*Is there a mother on earth who wouldn't give up everything to hear this?*

It was real. In an instant, I felt returned to my old life: walking in a park on a path of perfect symmetry, I had my balance again, with Kristen's small hand in one of mine and Amanda's small hand in my other. Their warmth and tenderness ran through me like a smooth river. Would it continue?

## NEIGHBOR
April 12, 2005   Dream

*In the library, I meet with my Chinese psychiatrist. We look for privacy, moving from one table or nook to another. The Chinese doctor is making a paper origami dog for me. When he reaches to hand it to me, the dog runs away. But I catch it. The session is nearly over and I ask for two more minutes. He agrees, and I explain my pain is unrelenting and I may collapse or die from it. His reply is, "You must find a way to release or relieve this stress." We make no further appointments.*

One morning, my Buddhist neighbor-philosopher asked me how I was doing.

"Not too well. I think I need help," I said.

He walked into his house and returned with the business card of a psychiatrist. "You can trust him," he said quietly.

A few weeks later, I had an appointment with the psychiatrist in Westwood.

"Can you tell me why you are here?" he asked at our first meeting.

"Will I survive the loss of my daughter, Amanda?" I asked,

"Why did you wait two years before coming in? If you had a broken bone, you'd fix it, wouldn't you?"

"I don't know if I can be fixed. I don't know if I want to be fixed," I replied.

My mother had insisted I get professional help. So did the rest of my family. Dr. Winston didn't unnerve me, so I returned on a regular basis.

I asked, "Will I ever get through this? Will it ever end?"

"You can't push it away; you can't fight it; you can't deny it; it becomes part of you," he answered. The loss will be there forever. Let's see if the pain will.

November 24, 2003   Dream
*She and I drive into green-forested mountains. We ride in a yellow convertible next to a cascading river.*

*Soon, we are speeding through the rural countryside on a dark night with some crossroads, no lights, and nearly meeting with an accident.*

*Obeying the rules, problems are solved together telepathically. Afraid if I speak—if I question or say a word—she'll vanish. I am careful not to prod, nudge, or behave in a way to damage the fragile dimensions binding us together. She leads; I follow.*

I knew fighting my grief was getting me nowhere.

He introduced me to the concept of metabolizing my daughter's loss: fear of the unknown, intellectualization, critical thinking, and the futility of it all have taken me years to absorb. His concept of metabolizing, I began to understand. This was a glimmer of hope.

Intellectualization was an important part of my process. My survival also depended on critical thinking and analysis.

## APPREHENSION

Despite some reservations, Bob told me being an ambassador with OneLegacy was helpful for him; it gave him a sense of purpose and kept Amanda alive. I had no interest and didn't want to be involved. He believed an extraordinary gift had been given to our family.

His way of keeping Amanda alive was by speaking to hospital staff. He would begin, "I need your help to tell you Amanda's story. Please close your eyes just for a moment and imagine my words: 'You have just entered Riverside Regional Hospital and passed through adult intensive-care unit's locked steel doors, looking for Amanda's room.'"

His presentation gave a rare look into a family making the decision to donate or not. Either choice was forever—irrevocable.

With trepidation, I attended OneLegacy's ambassador training program, including workshops, volunteer activities, and short presentations as a donor mom. Initially, I felt numb—as if I were reading a script. Little by little, the words became mine. Speaking in radio interviews, in video shoots, in focus groups, and to high-school classes was valuable in my new life and kept Amanda within me.

We always speak of her in the present tense. Always. Donation was the right thing to do.

With time, I became more comfortable in presentations to medical staff and students at UCLA and USC. Seven years earlier, I would have run out the door in fright as I did at the first Dove Ceremony. Our culture addresses death and dying in archaic and unhealthy ways. People are uncomfortable talking about these topics. Moorpark College has the only curriculum dedicated to death and dying. Dr. Julie Campbell's class provided Bob and me with the opportunity to help change; students were offered a voice for their stories and experiences. We were always surprised by their enthusiasm.

The first student to raise a hand showed the most courage. Without exception, the rest of the class now felt safe to share his or her story. Even after the bell rang, students stayed to ask questions and talk more. We saw their eyes opened and their taboos shed at that moment, in that place, on that day.

## HEART
August 25, 2006   Dream

*Arriving at my "new" home, I feel terribly guilty for returning after such a long period. Amanda's in second grade and is dressed in her school uniform, bundled in a scarf and knit cap. Who dressed her? It's night, and she stands in the frame of the front door, stepping down the porch stairs. She turns back to look up at me as if for a good-bye kiss and then quickly runs down the walkway. I run to catch her but can't. She's gone on to a dark, paved street, slickened by rain in this dreary night. An old-fashioned vintage car waits for her while three strangers lean against the car—all dressed in black wool topcoats and hats waiting quietly, like black crows on a wire. I allow it and look on wistfully. A streetlamp illuminates the midnight, moonless scene.*

*Back in the house, her sister and I try to find something to do when all of a sudden Amanda bursts through the door and comes bouncing over to me. She does not speak aloud; nor do I. We both know not to. "Did you decide to cut school to be with me?" I ask. With a sweet, pale smile, she nods yes. An odd, comfortable feeling comes over the three of us, and we know the world is right again.*

A year and a half had passed since Amanda's death when I received a call out of the blue on a pleasant Santa Monica evening.

"Hi," my brother said. His voice sounded thin and different. "The recipient of Amanda's heart has died."

His words were like a body blow that knocked the wind out of me. He must have known what I was thinking as he said, "Wait. Don't think of this as though Amanda has died again."

He'd just received a call from Tenaya Wallace, OneLegacy's director of communications.

"Tenaya called me with the news; as we spoke, I had a clear picture in my mind. I said to Tenaya, 'This is very sad, but wait—six people have lived two years more; isn't that true?'"

"That's true," Tenaya responded.

"This is twelve years of life, that of an adolescent, given by Amanda," Bob replied to her.

"You are right. I have never thought about it this way," Tenaya paused.

When my brother Bob and I started writing this book, these five recipients had lived an additional seven years. With Amanda's heart resulting in another two years, it was a total of thirty-seven years—the equivalent of one adult life.

Jim received one of Amanda's kidneys and her pancreas. Now, he and his wife, Ellen, have fourteen grandchildren. Before his transplant at Loma Linda Hospital, they had none.

May 1, 2008   Dream
KELP

*There's a sense of drowning, which has its own allure, looking up at a watery ceiling, hoping for a rope, reaching for a hand to grasp. Swimmers, boats, waves, and sunlight were swirling above so far away. Free falling, struggling, drowning—I felt as if I were being caught in oceans of kelp, knowing I couldn't fight my way out. Lying still, I allowed the kelp forest to untangle. Currents carried me to a new surface—not the familiar, safe, clear, firm, oxygenated, warm, and sunny surface. That's gone for good.*

## LUCK

A long line of faceless candidates still wait, and wait, and wait for donations. There was randomness about the organ checklist when we made our decisions at 3:00 a.m. in a dark conference room. We were deprived of sleep and were confused and frightened. These profound decisions in the worst of times were reduced to little more than checkmarks on paper forms. In fact, that's all they were. These checkmarks were turned into electronic signals fed into the ether of a national database. It was as though the gods would decide who would see again, who would breathe again, or who would walk again.

Was it luck of the draw? Was it a crapshoot?

Amanda had no throw of the dice. The odds were against her. I did my best.

My brother told me, "I was at a OneLegacy event and saw a larger-than-life picture of a six-year-old girl with brunette bangs and large brown eyes who'd received a cornea transplant.

Driving home, the image of this little girl hit me so hard I cried and had to pull off the road. What struck me was a piercing, stabbing guilt. I felt I hadn't done enough that night in the conference room. It still haunts me."

Our decision to donate was set forever and could not be reversed. Another person had to die for this six-year-old to ever have had a chance to see again.

## STONY PEAK

Amanda resides in a small pine box engraved with a spirited pony and locked with a brass clasp. She rests on my living-room bookcase, next to my mother. When I pass by, that spirited pony seems to follow me. We should not be too far from each other; place matters.

Although the winds change, a green weeping willow atop a hill reserves a place in the cemetery for Amanda. The deep shade protects her. Huge boulders, clear streams, and crevasses inhabited by rabbits and an occasional fox are her neighbors... who sometimes trot around the cemetery at nite. A red-tailed hawk soars above, like a sentry. From Amanda's knoll, mountains and rocks jut skyward, known by locals as Stony Peak. As children, we climbed these rocky pillars. I couldn't have imagined three generations of my family would someday be buried so close. Grandpa Robert, Aunt Ruby, and Amanda lie nearby. A Spanish mission church overlooks them.

Place matters. Forty-six years ago, our father died in a jeep accident in the mountains north of Paso Robles, California. He and my mother were returning from Wounded Knee at the Sioux Indian Reservation in South Dakota. At his funeral, our family chose to read an excerpt from Chief Joseph of the Nez Perce: "From where the sun now stands, I will fight no more forever", and another quote from Crazy Horse: "My home is where my dead lie buried."

April is the month Amanda left us. T. S. Eliot wrote, "April is the cruellest month."

## THE MALLARDS

Our writing was difficult and came slowly. In May, several years after the loss of Amanda, my brother and I took refuge on Saturdays in my backyard to write our story. We sat at the patio table, shaded by a blue canvas umbrella. Coffee and pastries fortified us. We took out paper and pens. Santa Monica's beach weather was warm and breezy. A palette of flowers bloomed—purple lobelia, white-faced jasmine, blue agapanthus, red geraniums, and fuchsia-colored bougainvillea.

Mallards and their ducklings crash-landed in the swimming pool and paddled about. Spanky and Cranky, Amanda's cats, poised at the edge of the water, waiting patiently for a feathered meal. With the flick of a webbed foot, each mallard paddled away to safety.

Writing inspired us, but like the *Myth of Sisyphus*, often it was like pushing a boulder uphill—tedious and frustrating. Two hours drained us. Bob would get cranky and look at his watch.

"I need to stop. I have to go. No more for today."

He had an hour's drive each way from his home in Thousand Oaks.

## JULY

June rolled by. It was a hot July. My birthday, July 1st, came before Amanda's.

I found myself saying aloud, "7/11/77, 7/11/77, 7/11/77, 7/11/77, 7/11/77, 7/11/77, 7/11/77, 7/11 /77, 7/11/77, 7/11/77, 7/11/77, 7/11/77, 7/11/77, 7/11/77, 7/11/77, 7/11/77, 7/11/77, 7/11/77, 7/11/77, 7/11/77, 7/11/77."

I couldn't stop repeating the date 7/11/77—the month, day, and year Amanda was born in Santa Monica Hospital, in Santa Monica, California.

CHAPTER 3

# An Invitation

IN MIDSUMMER OF 2011, ONELEGACY'S communications specialist, Stephanie, called with exciting news.

Amanda had been invited to "ride" OneLegacy's float in the 2012 Rose Parade. Amanda and other donors would be honored with their own flower-covered Floragraphs, memorial portraits. My feelings were a mix of honor, pride, confusion, joy, and anxiety. It was surreal. It was magical.

Would I be reunited with Amanda? Would I fall apart ?

*Is it Pandora's box?*

I welled up. My hands shook as I hung up the phone.

## KEYS AND LETTERS

Cleaning out my closet in the early fall of 2011, I unexpectedly found boxes of Amanda's medical records, credit cards, utility bills, driver's license, canceled checks, CDs, unpaid cell-phone bills, birthday cards, her passport, and personal letters. On her to-do list on a grease board, she had written a note for her boy-friend, Mike. "Get duplicate set of keys for Michael." There would be no keys—stinging proof of the unfinished business of her life.

Also hidden in the back of the closet was an envelope holding letters from two recipients. I looked at them and set them aside. Later, sitting at my dining room table, I read them. The writers expressed their profound gratitude for their extended lives with families, telling of newborn grandchildren, vegetable gardens, flowers, and trees. Having no recollection of ever replying to these letters, I was stunned to find copies of my responses mailed seven years earlier. What else had I set-aside during the past seven years?

## RECIPIENTS

In October, OneLegacy's family services specialist asked, "Would you like to meet them?"

Someone who gardens must be a nurturing person; someone with lots of grandchildren is surely a family man. She'd sparked my curiosity. My brother and I agreed to a meeting.

Tenaya Wallace, OneLegacy communications director, wanted to videotape the meetings.

"This is going to be an historic event," she said. "Of course, donor families and recipients have met but not after so many years. You have a unique perspective."

Having had no communication in the past seven years did seem unusual. "Let's meet!"

## ROOM TONE

Tenaya wanted to document the events as they unfolded. An initial meeting with documentary filmmaker Matt Radecki was scheduled at my house.

After arriving promptly, he assembled a "movie studio" in the living room. He placed cameras, adjusted lights, plugged in monitors, balanced reflectors, and covered the floor with blue mattresses. He even checked for "room tone."

I sat on the living-room couch. A vase of yellow spring flowers was behind me. Through the front windows, liquid amber trees stood tall, turning green and leafy. Tenaya offered a box of tissues and asked us specific questions. Bob teared up, barely getting through his interview. His tears continued well after the cameras were turned off.

"This was a good tear fest," Tenaya said.

I was afraid I would be unable to either explain or describe my feelings. There were no words.

Matt returned for a second shoot to complete the video. We watched him quickly unpack his cargo of equipment. His studio set was ready.

Matt started taping. Trying to describe my loss, I came up empty-handed. As Matt walked through the house, he shot a photo of Amanda atop a desk in the den.

In front of the garage door, Amanda's English riding saddle rested on a wooden stand as though in ready position. The saddle's stitched leather was still smooth, polished, and soft to the touch. With taping completed for the day, Matt meticulously packed his equipment into the trunk. He drove off in his studio on wheels. Red-veined maple leaves in autumn's gold colors scattered, crackled, and swirled, chasing after his car as he disappeared around the corner.

## FACE-TO-FACE

In November, before Thanksgiving, we met with the kidney and pancreas recipients. That morning, Matt, Bob, and I began the day at my house. I felt the harsh reality of meeting them face-to-face. Collecting a few of Amanda's photos to take wasn't easy for me. The driver of our town car arrived in professional attire. He opened the door of the black sedan. Matt took the front passenger seat for better camera angles and faced us. Pointing his camera, he began to tape our nervous and tentative conversation as we navigated the Santa Monica freeway. To other drivers, we appeared to be ordinary commuters.

At the corporate offices of OneLegacy in downtown Los Angeles, we were escorted through security doors to the small office reserved for the meeting. Tenaya directed us to form a receiving line. The door opened, and the recipient and his wife entered, followed by Matt. We exchanged names and hugs. Tenaya assigned seats at a round table. We weren't sure what to do next.

"Jim, please tell us a little about yourself and your family," Bob said.

"I was an air traffic controller for years but was forced to quit the job I loved when diagnosed with diabetes. I battled this disease for twenty-five years," he answered.

I thought to myself: for those same twenty-five years, Amanda lived with exuberance and a passion for horses.

Ellen, Jim's wife, said, "I don't know if I should have brought this, or if you would feel uncomfortable looking at this picture of Jim's recent hospitalization."

"Yes, I want to see it."

Ellen explained that during a family visit to the Midwest, Jim contracted a life-threatening infection, and his doctors placed him in an induced coma. The physicians were astonished that Amanda's kidney and pancreas were unaffected and said her organs were functioning just like those of a twenty-five-year-old.

"Jim got the very best," I said. We all chuckled. Our laughter helped us settle in.

A close look at the photo showed that he appeared weak and frail in his hospital bed, connected to a maze of tubes and monitors. The image yanked me back for a split second to Amanda's hospital bed, where she was connected to a labyrinth of tubes, monitors, and other machines. Ellen, children, and grandchildren, packed two and three deep, surrounded him. So many newborn babies had arrived. Ellen, with her big smile and curly hair, was the leader of the pack. Though Jim was comatose, she led the family in prayers and songs. Sitting at the table this day, he was the picture of health. His sky-blue eyes sparkled as he looked at Ellen with pride.

"I'm grateful beyond words and feel honored to consider Amanda as part of our family," Jim said.

"Are you taking good care of Amanda?"

"I am trying to be a good caretaker. I never miss my doctor's checkups. I eat well, exercise regularly, and tend to the family garden," he replied with humility and a sense of reverence.

Jim walked in today as a faceless organ recipient. Now, he is Amanda's caretaker; my daughter's in good hands. What a blessing. These lovely people were no longer the lucky ones—the faceless recipients I had resented for too long. Jim and Ellen have lives, families, homes, gardens, churches, and a marriage.

"This was like an arranged marriage. Neither of us asked for it, but it has turned out to be a great match," I said. We all laughed.

Tenaya sensed our meeting was coming to a close and suggested we all go to lunch in the cafeteria.

"Have you ever felt any guilt about receiving Amanda's organs?" Bob asked Jim over sandwiches and sodas.

Upon reflection, Jim answered, "Yes, it was hard to know and realize someone's life was lost while I gained mine."

Afternoon had arrived. It was time to leave. Jim and Ellen had a two-hour drive to their home in Lancaster in the high desert. Our hugs were warm; cameras snapped away. We exchanged addresses and phone numbers and followed up with more hugs and handshakes. We let go and waved good-bye.

We were tired from the intensity of the day. "Thank God we don't have to drive," Bob said. In the choking traffic, we sat back and reflected on a day so surprising, enlightening, and spiritual. "There was *no* Pandora's box. There was *no* Pandora's box," I exclaimed, almost in disbelief.

## LA FAMILIA

In early December, Kari, coordinator for OneLegacy, scheduled a meeting with the liver recipient in the large conference room on the fourth floor of OneLegacy.

Arturo, his wife, and their five adult children, two of whom brought their spouses, joined us.

As with Jim and Ellen, Arturo's family had gathered in a separate room for a briefing. Kari opened the conference-room doors. Bob and I quickly formed a receiving line. We welcomed Amanda's liver recipient. Arturo, a tall and hefty man, was the obvious patriarch of the family. Tentatively, he handed me a beautiful bouquet of fresh flowers and then gave me a big bear hug. His wife, Mila—short for Hermila—was next in line, followed by Lorena, Blanca, Arturo Jr., Adriana, and Monica. Tears and emotions enveloped all of us.

After an awkward pause, Bob suggested, "Why don't we sit on both sides of the long conference table so we can see and hear each other?"

I sat at the head of the table, with Arturo and his wife on my left and Bob on my right. The children took the remaining seats. Kari, as an observer, took a chair at the back of the room. The formation was balanced. The large panel of windows revealed a panorama of Los Angeles' skyline at its best. We settled in for our meeting.

Monica was the spokesperson for the family. Bob, fluent in Spanish, spoke to Arturo and Hermila in their native language.

He also translated for me, conveying that Arturo and Mila were born in the same pueblo in Zacatecas, Mexico, and married there. They immigrated to the United States, became citizens, and raised a family in Southern California.

Something Mila would like to do, in honor of her husband's transplant miracle, is travel back to Zacatecas to give thanks to God for her husband's life.

"Many times I wanted to return to Zacatecas, to pray to Saint of Child Jesus (Santo Nino de Atocha) for Amanda's gift to Arturo. Zacatecas, located in Central Mexico, has a long history of mining with a unique combination of European and Mexican architecture. These stone quarries are among the finest in Mexico and are used by sculptors the world over. Zacatecas has an artist's soul," Mila told us in Spanish.

"My father is a quiet man of few words. We often speak for him. The baseball cap he's wearing today never leaves his head," Monica said.

They all nodded in agreement. They had noticed changes in Arturo's behavior since his transplant.

"Now, he likes to eat chips and fried chicken, which he never did before. He especially likes to do this while watching a ball game on TV," Monica said.

"On her Monday nights off from work, Amanda came home to do her laundry. She'd lie down on the living-room couch munching chips, eating chicken, and watching the TV while the washing machine whirred in the background," I said.

*Is Amanda's spirit alive in Arturo beyond just her organ?*

## ARTURO'S DREAM

"Arturo is now more expressive in his opinions and ideas," family members said.

Quietly, Arturo told us, "During my operation, I had a dream I've kept secret from everyone, including Mila, until today."

Having always shared everything, his family gasped in disbelief. "What happened, Papa? Why have you waited until today to tell us about your dream after seven years?"

A flurry of questions filled the room. His subtle grin was his answer.

"During my surgery, I dreamed I was in a special place, very high up. I was walking on the tops of tall trees and then I reached behind to find a small hand in mine, the hand of a young blond-haired girl. It was a foggy night, and her long hair flowed as we crossed the tops of willow trees. She led me to a different place. She was taking me to a good place. It was the right thing."

Arturo's voice was soft.

The story astonished them. Monica blurted, "What, Dad? You never told us this before."

Mila, Lorena, and Arturo Jr. shook their heads. Neither Arturo nor his family had known anything about Amanda's gender, age, name, or circumstances of her accident. For seven years, she'd been anonymous. Amanda was the girl in his dream.

*Were Arturo and Amanda meant to meet this way?*

She was safe with Arturo.

"Now Amanda is one of our sisters," Lorena declared. She belongs.

Monica and Arturo gestured to me. "Would you like to feel Amanda's liver?"

"Yes, I would."

When I laid my hand on the left side of his abdomen, a few of those present burst out in giggles. They graciously told me I was touching the wrong side. They pointed to his right side. We all laughed. "You know Amanda's liver better than me," I said, red-faced. We all had a great laugh.

"Isn't it time for lunch? Aren't you all hungry?" Kari asked.

In the cafeteria, we combined tables so we could eat together as a "family."

After ordering sandwiches, salads, potato chips, and dessert, Mila led us in prayer as we held hands. Starting a tradition in honor of Amanda and Arturo, we all ate a few chips.

Our conversation took us back to Zacatecas and then returned us to our lunch. We felt closer as the day came to an end. It gave me a feeling of contentment and was all I could have hoped for.

Big hugs, *hasta luegos*, and no good-byes closed the day.


## THE TURKS AND CAICOS

Early in the morning of Saturday, December 3, we all met at the chilly float pavilion in Pasadena. This huge warehouse was the temporary home for the construction of flower-covered behemoths, encased by metal frames that seemed to reach the sky. Volunteers worked high in the scaffolding, fluttering and humming like bees. Bob, his sons—my nephews Santos and Adrian—our family friend Paola, recipients Jim and Ellen, as well as Arturo and his family arrived wearing long coats and scarves. Kenny, Amanda's sister, was in Santa Rosa. I felt numb but appreciated the long drives everyone had made.

We were escorted through the maze of steel scaffolding to find ourselves surrounded by a sea of powder-blue T-shirts with large black letters stenciled on the back saying, "Donate Life, Done Vida."

We made our way through the ocean of blue to land at our table with Amanda's picture mounted on a pedestal for all to see. That was our island, and we were now part of the sea of blue. I studied Amanda's features up close and ran my hand across her cheek. Her Floragraph was rich in color and alive and seemed to reach out to me. This graphic likeness was more like a blueprint when I realized her blond hair, green eyes, rosy cheeks, and pink lips had been color-coded into the image. There were many other donor families, some coming from as far away as the Turks and Caicos,working on Floragraphs..

At the center of our table was her blueprint surrounded by little pots of paint, glue, dried lavender chrysanthemums, dried black seeds, and dried wheat-colored grasses.

My imagination sprinkled fairy dust in a circle. Suddenly, Amanda was next to me, chattering away. I was awash with that warm, confident feeling I was used to.

At our table, we shared family stories and some laughter and got to know one another even more.

"Please pass the paint, some glue, those small brushes, and a pot of wheatgrass. I'm working on Amanda's hair," Adrian said.

Paola replied, "Be careful. I just completed her eyes."

When it was finished, I walked the Floragraph to an adjacent table.

Paola introduced Amanda to John's mother. She had just finished putting the last touches on John's Floragraph. We mothers agreed, "Amanda and John would have liked each other."

We looked at each other and chuckled. It was great fun to imagine what could have been.

Amanda's floragraph was alive with fresh seeds, grasses, and dried flowers. Carefully, I ran my fingers across Amanda's cheek as her mischievous smile reflected back at me.

In the icy-cold pavilion, we wore scarves, mittens, coats, and sweaters. The behemoth floats, stilled moored at their docks, would be brought to life in the next few days with colorful flowers and seeds.

## GALA EVENTS

As guests of OneLegacy, we checked into the Pasadena Sheraton on December 29. The day was picture-perfect with clear blue skies set against the Angeles Crest Mountains. The next few days were filled: a gala in a grand ballroom, a morning brunch in the hotel, and float judging in the pavilion.

Before the gala event, we all settled in and had a light lunch and returned to our rooms to get ready for the evening.

At the front door of the giant ballroom, two pixie-dressed girls greeted us. They escorted us to our table, which was beautifully decorated with a bright bouquet of flowers. The evening was devoted to honoring the donors whose Floragraphs would ride the float. Several hundred families quietly in awe, filed into the ballroom as we had.

As they caught their breath, we heard waves of oohs and ahhs.

A hypnotic light show of vivid neon colors cast rhythmic geometric shapes on the walls and ceilings.

Social niceties seemed unnecessary. Everyone knew why we were here and what linked us together. We shared our stories with ease. I felt I belonged here. It was comforting.

At our table, another mother sat next to Bob. She had traveled all the way from New York. The woman revealed to Bob that she had lost her daughter in an accident just two weeks earlier.

"Her story knocked the wind out of me. I told her how much courage she had to get on a plane and attend this event," Bob said to me.

As part of the tribute, photographs of the donors were projected on a giant screen at the front of the ballroom. All of a sudden, there was Amanda with her name and date of birth. Her magic smile gleamed. She looked directly at me.

"Hi, Mom," she said.

Then she was gone.

Photographs of the other donors followed.

## SCARVES AND MITTENS

Early the next morning, we arrived at the Rose Pavilion.

"What a beautiful blue sky," Bob said. It was another picture-perfect day. Above the huge arches on the Rose Bowl Stadium entrance, the big red rose emblem accentuated the majestic Angeles Crest Mountain in the background. Inside the cold pavilion, we wore scarves, mittens, and coats.

The completed floats were driven from their moorings to be judged. Outside, a sea of volunteers in powder-blue T-shirts embraced our float: "Seize the Day." Not a word was spoken; a spontaneous rhythm of hands softly clapping filled the air as the judges moved around the float. Emotions filled and bonded us all. The judges weren't immune.

"No other float in the parade was built by such a unique and pure community as ours," Tenaya whispered into my ear.

Bob, Adrian, Cousin Maureen, Cousin Nancy, and I dined at a cozy Italian restaurant. We had a champagne toast to Amanda. We returned to our hotel early because we needed to be in our bleacher seats by sunrise. Bob went down to Colorado Boulevard to take pictures of the crowds getting ready and bundling up for a cold night.

ROSE PARADE—January 1, 2012
Alarms went off. We climbed out of bed bleary-eyed. Our family collected in the lobby, and a blast of cold air completed our wake-up as we left the hotel.

Swept up in a growing river of people, we headed in the same direction down Colorado Boulevard. Jostling and bumping shoulders politely, we navigated this sea of people shrouded in morning fog. Donor families were given reserved bleacher seats. Surrounded by familiar faces, I was with my own kind and could speak with ease as though we already knew one another.

As far as the eye could see, motorcycle police cleared the last of the people meandering on Colorado Boulevard. Each side of the boulevard was packed, but the street was empty. What a strange sight.

# BABY JACOB

The fog lifted magically to reveal another cloudless ocean-blue sky. Warmed by the morning sun, we removed our hats and gloves.

In the distance, drums rolled and bugles and trumpets heralded the parade's beginning. Around the corner of Colorado Boulevard, the giant floats emerged as if awakened by the vibrant calls of the marching bands. Oohs and ahhs resounded from the bleachers. The parade came alive and took over the street for a few hours. Then it was gone forever.

Amanda's float was scheduled to stop in front of us. The seats had been assigned to ensure we would be able to see our own Floragraphs. We snapped pictures and took part in that special moment. Amanda herself was part of the blue sky; flying kites were tethered to the float. With a radiance of color, she belonged to the world. Hers was the engine in the lives of Arturo and Jim. Arturo's dream, fresh in my mind, told me my daughter was in the caring hands of Arturo and his family, and Jim and Ellen.. Amanda had a place, a purpose, beyond my need to keep her. Heaven had a community of beautiful souls, many of whom I "met" that day.

One Floragraph of smiling Baby Jacob, a two-year-old donor, was next to Amanda on the float's banner. I had hoped she would live a full life and have children of her own. She loved children. In my imagination, she smiled at her baby—Baby Jacob—as they traveled side by side.

*Spin and die,*
*to live again a butterfly.*

*—CHRISTINA ROSSETTI*

My eyes brimmed with hot tears. I watched in wonderment. Their faces faded away as they neared the parade's end.

## DAY'S END

New Year's Day ended with an elegant dinner at a Brazilian restaurant. Our family clinked crystal glasses of champagne to toast Amanda, the New Year, and our futures.

Sheets of gray rain met us the next morning at checkout. Knowing this might be our families' last time together, we enjoyed brunch in the hotel's dining room. Our conversations were layered with an unspoken sense of sadness.

Gathering our suitcases, we headed to the lobby. We patted the heads of Lyle and Henry, two show-stopping dogs who caught Frisbees in midair while jumping into a swimming pool on their special float. Cousin Maureen in her taxi headed to LAX for her flight to Michigan. In the downpour we drove Cousin Nancy to the train station for her trip to Apple Valley in the Mojave Desert. The rest of us headed in our separate directions: San Fernando Valley, Thousand Oaks, Ventura, and Santa Monica.

We headed home after leaving Nancy; the car's windshield wipers splashed across the front window. My mother was sitting next to me in the front seat. I asked her, "Mother, do you think Amanda will ever return?"

"No, Liz, as long as you feel her radiance, she will be with you till the day you die."

May 20, 2011    Dream
*Gliding effortlessly underwater, I could see forever through the crystal-clear turquoise lagoon. Swimming forward, the coral sand beneath was radiant.*

Every once in a while, lying in my bed on a cool, clear early morning, I hear, "Hi, Mom." It is Amanda. It *is* Amanda.

# CHAPTER 4

# Amanda

FRIDAY, THE WEEKEND OF APRIL 18, 2003, the sky in Nevada's vast desert was cloudless and blue. Amanda, my twenty-five-year-old daughter, and I flew into McCarran International Airport in Las Vegas to watch the World Cup Equestrian Competition. In recent months, having spent less time together, I jumped at the opportunity to be with my daughter for the entire weekend. Checking into the Mirage Hotel, our little party of two went straight to our suite and settled in. Indulging myself, I ordered room service and took a bubble bath. Amanda unpacked and took the mahogany-walled elevator downstairs to meet her boyfriend in the lobby. He'd flown in for the weekend.

Good days were upon us as the sun rose slowly.

Amid blistering heat, silvery shimmering mirages, and rolling tumbleweeds as far as our eye could see, we drove our rented car to the stadium.

Amanda was excited for her firsthand look at the best warm-blooded horses from seven continents. Celebrities in their own right, they had pedigrees, passports, and birthplaces from England, Belgium, Germany, South America, Canada, Spain, Argentina, France, and the United States. Weeks earlier, these two-thousand-pound animals had been crated, lifted by crane, and rolled onto the cargo floor of a specially designed jumbo 777. In attendance were personal groomers and veterinarians; cargo and immigration officials were at their side. They monitored safety, administered special diets of hay and water, calmed the priceless cargo, and prepared documents for customs and quarantines.

Since she was three, Amanda was fascinated by ponies. At her birthday picnic in Griffith Park that year, she tugged and tugged my hand. "Mommy, Mommy, I want to do that." Amanda pointed to small ponies tethered to a pole inside a wood-railed ring.

"OK."

Snugly strapped and buckled in the saddle, confidently she gripped the horn. She had to be cajoled off her "whissy" when the brief ride was over. She asked to go again and again and again.

After all, wasn't it her birthday picnic?

By twelve, Amanda had competition in her blood. She was a twig of a girl, plucky for her age, but her appetite for riding was insatiable. Twice weekly, in my "divorce car"—a rickety gray station wagon—we drove PCH (Route 1), then managed a steep winding, unpaved dirt road, with several *arroyo secos* and creeks.

An original 1875 Franciscan Mission bell marked a graveled parking area near the large paddock on the far side of the weathered barn. On a small hill overlooking the ranch, her trainer hollered "more leg Amanda, less heel," as Amanda trotted around the ring. Her ponytail and the horse's tail swished and bounced together. Nibbling on a sandwich from our sack lunch, I was under an ancient tree laden with pomegranates, which shaded me—fruit at my fingertips.

Later, Amanda's grandma, Janet, a competitive equestrian in her college years, joined us at the event in Julian near Temecula during a severe heat wave. At a local livery store, Grandma Janet bought the remaining sombrero—so big I almost lost sight of her. Grandma Janet didn't want to miss anything, so we hurried on. A featherweight herself, she almost disappeared under her sombrero embroidered with green cacti and mariachis. Wearing her tightly tied hat, she walked straight to the arena. *What is it,* I wondered, *that made me feel this moment was so remarkable it must be captured on film? Was it the blinding sun saying take it before it's gone?* I snapped the photo.

Soon after, in another event in Las Vegas, it was different for Amanda; this time she was an observer, not a participant. Inside McCarran Conference Arena, we located our seats in a packed stadium; the rarefied atmosphere was palpable. Sitting side-by-side, shoulders rubbing, squeezed in, our eyes turned toward the center of the arena; the competition began. We listened; we watched. Taking it all in, she was biting at the bit. Smiling with confidence, I knew Amanda imagined herself as a world-class competitor.

"Mom, trust with the horses has to be earned daily. When you've cleaned and dressed them, braided their tail, brushed their mane, and cleaned their shoes, the relationship builds. Routine and dependability lead to the next level; they are trained as athletes. Guided over low rails, rewarded for jumping six-foot fences... months and years of constant practice to build trust takes everything I have."

Even in the rafters, our stadium seats gave us a clear view across the entire arena. High above us, a massive, retractable steel dome shielded the crowd from searing desert heat. The dome created a world unto itself, with a sense of security and comfort inside this cavern. All were here: trainers, riders, owners, grooms, families, and aficionados. The aroma of hot dogs and popcorn drifted in the air. The fast tempo and staccato sounds of violins, trumpets, and guitars from the mariachi band had people standing, clapping, and stomping their feet. The four-legged champions stood at the ready for the six timed elite events.

With a professionally designed and well-groomed sandy floor, the courses, turns, hurdles, ponds, and shrubbery met strict requirements of international regulations. Each event station was elaborately decorated with flowers, greenery, banners, and flags. Elegant pageantry—pomp and circumstance—was steeped in

English tradition. Before competition, each rider had walked the course, counting the exact number of steps their horse should take between each station. Being off by one or two steps risked time penalties. The start time was signaled by the blare of official trumpets. The horses' ribbons with their countries' colors fluttered and flapped in the wind as they thundered by.

How many times had I seen Amanda carefully count each step between stations at her events? Her focus was 100 percent on step counts and jump sequences.

"I have to concentrate, Mom. You can be anxious for both of us."

The race began with hooves pounding, digging into the soft dirt, leaving wakes of twisting, churning dust, like dust devils across the desert landscape. We barely glimpsed the shiny, varnished hooves galloping from hurdle to hurdle, fence to fence, pond to pond. The highest six-foot jumps drew total silence in the stadium. Reins were pulled tightly for smooth landings. Hooves cut deep into their targeted marks; an audible sound of relief wafted from the crowd watching a safe landing of the horse and the rider. The only sounds were nostrils snorting, teeth grinding, and jaws gaping, with spittle and foam flung out in lacy patterns.

"See that, Mom? That's me one day," she said, pointing down at the arena.

One arm looped through hers; with the other I grabbed the box of popcorn. We shared cold sodas with our group like a familial picnic.

With infinite patience, she tried to explain competition at the elite level. First, the horse's height is measured—by stacking one hand on top of the other from ground level up to the animal's ear. If a horse is being examined, one might ask, "How many hands it has?" Second, riders must follow rigid protocol; for example, starting before the trumpet sounds risked disqualification.

"I'll sum it up and put things in simple terms. The rider with the fastest time and the fewest penalties wins the event." I loved her for knowing I needed to hear the bottom line. Our grins seemed to spring out of nowhere—like crocuses in April, like mushrooms in rain, like sunflowers in sunlight.

During intermission, Amanda spotted two empty box seats adjacent to the arena floor. "Let's go sit there. You can see better; I can study a certain horse."

She held out her hand helping me down the steep bleachers. Her long nimble fingers, like those of a pianist, had the strength of a vise grip. We traversed tricky stairs finding empty seats. The vibration of their hooves shook our seats. Their hot sweat was unmistakable as they whipped by.

"Mom, I am gonna do this one day."

Nudging her shoulder with mine, I felt a little like one horse nuzzling another. Such fun. "Oh, enough, Mom. Let's watch."

Intermission over, Western-style barrel racing began. Gritty and ferocious, it's a wild fight to fly around barrels at breakneck speed without horse or rider pulling one another down into the dirt without crashing. The winners cut corners like a hot knife cuts butter.

"Amanda, I'd have done this if I'd grown up on a ranch or farm." Hell-bent to reach the finish line first, the rider and the horse threw caution to the wind. Intoxicated by the speed, I was thinking to myself, *Sure, I could have done that.* Ha!

At day's end she offered me her arm, and together we climbed the bleachers. Her patience and consideration touched me!

Was I that patient with my mother? What would my mother have said?

Leaving the air-conditioned stadium, we stepped outside and the hard-hitting heat punched us; mirages ribboned the desert's edges.

Late in the afternoon, at the hotel's boutique, Amanda, as usual, shopped at lightning speed, grabbing a pink sleeveless

T-shirt, which fit her lithe, muscled body perfectly. She turned heads.

*Where did this little angel come from?*

I found a loose turquoise blouse embroidered with green palm trees and silver sequins. A different choice, with a little sparkle to keep up with Amanda. Ha!

At the Mirage, I held up a Siegfried and Roy stuffed tiger. "No Mom. The pink T-shirt is enough."

It was uncanny how well she knew me when she said, "Mom, I know exactly what you're thinking. I know you really want to make me happy. I'm fine being here with you." We each had a special shirt to wear.

She had an intuitive sense of me. What a gift—this sunny girl.

Sunday afternoon, we zipped off to the airport for the one-hour flight back to LAX. Amanda offered up her tanned arm, wearing her new pink T-shirt. She was never embarrassed to have her mother in tow. I slipped my arm through hers, and we walked to the boarding area. My silver sequined blouse with green palm trees sparkled, as I did inside. Sounded corny but true.

We three were not always so happy, but we were solid. Our family endured divorce and normal potholes in the road. I worked full time: one daughter tried smoking, and the other tried weed. Both had boyfriends and a few broken hearts—usual trials of the teenage years—we always rose back to the surface. Like magnets, only two and a half years apart, the girls were closer than twins.

I loved to say "the girls." When they were little, Amanda would hold one of my hands and her sister held my other hand. In perfect balance with these two, I had my bearings.

Amanda had thick, long, shiny hair, and freckles splattered around her nose like honey spots. Her eyes were green-blue marbles, changing with the sky. Uncle Bob once said, "Amanda's no wallflower. She's in the game. She *is* the game."

# Big Mac

On the one-hour shuttle back to LAX, Amanda and I chatted. After a smooth flight and landing, we grabbed our luggage and walked outside to wait for Kristen. Amanda adored her. Lurching to the curb and chugging along, driving Amanda's beaten-up, white cabriolet on its last wheel, Kristen found us at the curbside. Giddy girls, we three were delighted to be together again, with smooches and wisecracks all around. "Kenny" was Kristen's nickname since childhood. Amanda knew how to weasel stuff from her sister, and she pleaded, "Please, please! I'm so hungry."

Amanda was skinny as a stick with an unending appetite; we all loved to feed her.

"OK, but that's all we'll stop for"—Kristen loved "doing" for her sister. She pretended in a begrudging, "Ooohhhh, allllll right."

Amanda threw a big, bouncy hug around Kristen's neck, knowing it was her real reward.

Love for hamburgers.

The girls dropped me off at home, racing away in a cloud of dust for Big Macs. Life goes on.

The sisters going for their junk food were as happy as though fairy dust had been sprinkled, as happy as clams at high tide.


# Back In LA

Feeling fevered and flushed, I didn't work Monday, April 21, staying home to rest and tackle a few small errands. Kristen had classes at college. Amanda planned to trailer one of the horses of the Malibu stable, where she worked. With another stable worker, they drove south to Temecula, about an hour north of San Diego. Galway Downs, in Temecula, was scheduled to host the next big competition, the Regional Cross Country. The

Malibu stable owner assigned Amanda a horse, and it needed a good workout to be ready. Competitors were coming from all over the western United States. Hot and sandy, Temecula was some fifty-five acres, an expansive ranch and grounds. This was a horse country, stretching across arid southern California. Although heated like an oven during the day, the land was cool and brisk at night.

One month earlier, at a Galway Downs competition in Temecula, on the winding, hilly course, spectators, owners, and onlookers ran, walked, drove golf carts, and raced from station to station to see which horse and rider would take the coveted trophies. In competition, Amanda and her horse, a team, each sported professionally braided ponytails. She wore a crisp, white riding blouse, breeches, polished black leather riding boots up to her knees, and a black velvet helmet. She wore black gloves and held a short, thin, braided-leather riding whip. Her horse was brushed to a silky sheen. A burnished English riding saddle was buckled on top of a dark-green blanket, cinched and ready. Her horse's hooves were varnished shiny black. Amanda's nails were polished shiny black. Trendy.

She rode high, pushing with ferocity; red-faced, sweating, and muscled—beating her own wings into the wind. They flew as if pursued by the devil himself. Horse and rider leaped the high rails, skimmed over ponds, zigzagged through clumps of tall green eucalyptus, scrambled up steep hills, and slip-slided down small knolls. Dust whorled. She'd beaten the devil.

Silhouetted against the electric-blue sky, her fist pumped to the heavens and her strong arms were raised in triumph. An unabashed smile crossed her face. At that second, she must have felt untouchable.

At day's end, all riders were summoned to the stage in the main ring. An official announced each competitors standing over a microphone. When awarding ribbons and trophies, they called their name and instructed them to move to the front.

I heard Amanda's name. She won first place!

Adjusting her seat, straightening her back, and arching and squaring her shoulders, Amanda moved forward to accept her large shiny Silver Bowl.

It read: "Amanda Katherine Seraphin, Division Champion, 1st Place, March 30, 2003."

Proudly holding up the engraved trophy above her head, she said, "I won this for my stable."


# THE EEL

Years earlier the three of us hopped the Caribbean Air and flew to the island of Saint Croix, a jewel in the Caribbean. The girls and I snorkeled for hours in an underwater coral reef preserve. Signs posted on sunken rocks had information on the fish and coral habitat; a few had warnings. Arrows on the rocks kept us to the trail.

During one dive, two unblinking beady eyes watched us closely. A large dull-green eel, wedged in a small crevice of brilliant-green, radiant-blue, and yellow corals, was protecting its home. The natural cadence of its gills drew in oxygenated seawater through its open mouth. Transfixing to watch; baring large white razor-sharp teeth, we kept our distance. Damsel fish were not intimidated, always hunting for food; these tiny creatures darted about the eel's head with a sense of immunity from certain death.

Surfacing, we shouted, "Did you see that eel staring right at us?"

"Did you see its eyes?"

"Did you see those sharp teeth?"

Our guide snapped pictures of us three wet-headed girls bobbing in the waves, masks and snorkels in tow, our smiles from ear to ear.

# MONDAY

That Monday afternoon, it was a relief to take the day off. Every Monday evening, Amanda and I had a comforting routine. She came over to relax. I did a load of her laundry, though she insisted she could do her own. "I like doing this for you." We ate, chatted, and chilled.

She'd worked as a nanny and babysat to make ends meet. Did she ever complain? Never.

As a horse trainer, Amanda loved to teach children how to ride. It wasn't a moneymaker; she managed a small apartment, a car, food, and two cats—Spanky and Cranky—who'd been rescued from abuse. Cranky had unusual eating habits. His food had to be placed underneath Amanda's bed. During the night, the crunching sound was Cranky eating his midnight dinner. After months of patient feeding, she coaxed Cranky out of his fear-imposed confinement. Bravo!

Monday, April 21, she would have trailered her horse back from Temecula to Malibu, turned around, made it to my house for dinner at 6:00 p.m., and bee lined to the couch. Earlier, I'd gone to Marie Calendar's. I bought two boxed chicken dinners with salad and corn bread—no burgers and fries for me. The world was right. Heading toward the exit, I collected the bags of hot food and extra napkins and paid the bill. I wanted to get home on time.

Then my cell phone rang.

I didn't want to answer it. *Well, I suppose I should. You never know.* I answered the call.

A Letter
April 2016

Dear Liz,

Actually, you come to mind so often for both Ellen and me but especially at this time of year. We can't believe it has been thirteen years since Amanda's passing, and I'm sure you miss her as much now as ever. I am so fortunate that you and your family (and Amanda) were willing to donate Amanda's organs to help others. Ellen and I just back from Alaska where we helped our oldest daughter, Beth, with the birth of her fourth girl and our fourteenth grandchild. All thirteen have been born since my transplant (thirteen years ago). We are truly blessed/grateful and are most fortunate to be able to enjoy all of our children. Amanda's kidney and pancreas are working perfectly and keeping me in great health. Please pass our love to Bob as well.

Sincerely,
Jim and Ellen

A Letter
October 2016

Dear Liz and Bob

We want you to know how much we appreciate you. We will always keep you close to our heart.

Amanda's legacy lives within our hearts. We thank you for allowing us to be part of your family. I carry Amanda's picture with me in my car. Her beautiful smile is imprinted forever.

Sincerely,
Lorena (Arturo's daughter)

P.S. Author's note: The Nunez family now has twelve grandchildren and four great grandchildren.

CHAPTER 5

# A Few Notes.......

YEARS LATER, I FOUND PEACE and renewal after experiencing such a dark place of violent disruption of life. The sudden shock of my loss was anesthetizing, immobilizing, and isolating as the world closed in.

My love for Amanda evolved into deepening gratitude for our 25 years together; for her donation to wonderful, deserving families; for becoming a link in the chain of life as I believe another might have done for her. Donation provided 72 years in total, the equivalent of one person's lifetime. This perspective hasn't come easy and wasn't linear, but it feels good to know this is a tangible legacy of hers.

Amanda's headstone, for fourteen years, still sits in a storeroom in Burbank, Ca. Why? I don't know. There's no explanation. Maybe I don't want to "upset the apple cart", change the order of things, or make it more official?

Amanda would say,.....

" Come on Mom, its not that big of a deal. I'll be out there with Grandpa Robert, Grandma Janet, Aunt Rubye, my father, on the sloping hill, we'll rest beneath the weeping willow tree, protected from winds and rains. We'll be surrounded by rocky canyons of Chatsworth where the foxes and rabbits come out at night and trot around the cemetery".

No decision yet, but we have these "talks".

Family and friends returned to their lives. Amanda's sister lives in Northern California and remembers her with photos, and flowers on a fireplace mantle. Amanda's photo hangs in her car on a gold chain so "they can travel around together". Santos and Adrian have finished school, and found jobs. Adrian lives in Brazil. Santos with his family in Ventura, Ca. Sister Christine returned home to New Orleans, La. Cousin Maureen passed on. Cousin Nancy is home in Grand Rapids, Michigan. Bob remains in Southern California. I'm in Los Angeles, still.

My feelings of anger long eluded me. Recently, when asked about this, I had a polaroid-like flash of a vision. Amanda's laying on the Hospital operating table. An anonymous doctor pries open her rib cage and chest. With gloved hands he reaches in and takes her heart and lungs. Like a broken violin string, I felt a stinging, snap of fury. "Amanda, how did this happen? A stranger performing something so intimate and invasive?" The feeling stung, then disappeared. She and I agreed to erase the photo from our minds, like chalk across a board; it worked. (We talk this way, sometimes.)

Like a visual diary, dreams matter as they chart the passing of time through events and emotions. Dreams are imaginative and creative, go beyond constraints of waking life. For example, from my dreams of loud explosive bombs dropping around me, I shuddered in fear. Later in another dream, I stood close to Amanda as she unfolded her iridescent angel wings, the lustrous, pinks and silvers, veined and sheer. Joy and relief flooded me knowing she'd found her way upward.

At times, I pleaded silently for Amanda to come to me in the night while I slept. At times she did. Even if I didn't remember the exact content of the dream, I "knew" as I awoke in the morning and felt the wonderful, "old" feeling of footing and balance; one daughter in each hand, my family of 3. I "knew" we were together, this is how she told me so... Einstein said he would rather have imagination than knowledge because knowledge is restricted and limited, imagination is not. Would he say it is the same for dreams?

Inspired by Arturo's dream of the willow tops, I wanted to know more about these majestic trees and their iconic status.

Through the ages, willows are found in literature, legend, art, folklore, and music and thus are anchored within our consciousness. With deep strong roots to provide an oasis of shade; they live near ponds, streams and lakes. In temperate climates, like China, they beautify palace courtyards and gardens, especially in a gentle breeze.

Some believe the willow is symbolic of immortality and re birth. Others see this majestic tree a symbol of grief, mysticism and superstition. I believe in both.

Tree experts believe the weeping willow's name came from raindrops falling off leaves of drooping branches resembling tears. The willow has a short life up to 30 years. Amanda's short life was 25 years.

In literature, in 1583 William Shakespeare, wrote "Willow Song", a song of great despair. In Hamlet, broken willow branches thrown in a river, foreshadow Ophelia drowning herself in that river. In art, weeping willows are painted in scenes commemorating a death, a funeral procession... notably in Victorian times. Medicinally, Cherokee Indians used willow bark tea as treatments for fever, pain and sore throat.

Willows are versatile. They renew the spirit. They are iconic. Remarkable willows: weeping for some, sheltering and comforting for others. I love the weeping willow, it has given both to me.

"We tell ourselves stories in order to live", the author said. Telling this story helped to sort things out, to look back on a narrative of growth and survival; to discover how and where we've landed; to be liberated.

Amanda exists, in a different way, as her grand mother said, "As long as you feel her radiance, she'll be with you always. And, she is.

*"When a great tree falls,*
*peace comes slowly*
*and irregularly over time."*[1]

MAYA ANGELOU

---

1 Adapted from the poem "When Great Trees Fall".

## ACKNOWLEDGMENTS

WITH ALL OUR GRATITUDE, WE *want to thank those who were indispensable, gracious, and encouraged us to tell this story.*

*John Cantando, MD, and Javed Siddiqi, MD, DPhil (Oxon), FRCSC, Riverside Regional Hospital, California, whose medical expertise was invaluable; even more so was the fact they shared their hearts and souls.*

*Gregg Smith, transplant coordinator, Los Angeles, California.*

*Tenaya Wallace, Communications Coordinator, OneLegacy, Los Angeles, California.*

*Matt Radecki, documentary filmmaker, Los Angeles, California.*

*Reinhard Teichmann, PhD, and Magdalena Teichmann, Ventura, California.*

*Julie Campbell, PhD, professor of the Death and Dying class at Moorpark College, California.*

*Yuri Hueda, translator, assistant professor, Mexico City.*

*Jan Taylor, consultant, Ventura, California.*

Special thanks to Tom Mone CEO of OneLegacy for authorizing the use of this video.

*To view the 8 minute award-winning documentary*
**Amanda's Caretaker,** *go to* HYPERLINK **https://vimeo.com/ 148923682.**

Authors' contact information: saemer02@mail.com

Made in the USA
Las Vegas, NV
28 August 2024

94537418R10049